Two Truths and a Lie

a memoir written & performed by
Scott Turner Schofield

foreword by Judith Halberstam

Homofactus PRESS

Published in 2008 by Homofactus Press, L.L.C
www.homofactuspress.com

copyright © 2001–2008 by Scott Turner Schofield

Printed in the United States of America

ISBN: 978–0–9785973–2–0

1. Transgender writings, American. 2. Transgender—United
States—Drama. 3. Monodramas. 4. Monologues. I. Scott Turner
Schofield II. Judith Halberstam

book design © 2008 by Jay Sennett
cover design © 2008 by Charlie Burnett

To my family and my teachers.

Table of Contents

Sweet Tea and The Queer Art of Digression: Scott Turner Schofield's Two Truths and a Lie
by Judith Jack Halberstam

Let me begin with my own two truths and a lie.

I love live performance! I hate live performance!
Scott Turner Schofield will change your life...

Ok, as for the lie: I generally do not love live
performance, especially anything that involves
nudity, audience participation or the singing of 80's
pop songs. But as my friends tell me, I am a guy who
"hates too much," and so every now and then I open
myself up to the things I think I cannot tolerate.
Mostly I walk away confirmed in my opinions, but
that was before Scott Turner Schofield. When Scott
performed "Debutante Balls" at USC in 2006, I went
along with my gender studies class to the
performance. Two hundred mostly straight college
kids sat entranced through the evening, hanging on
every line, sipping every Dixie cup of sweet tea that
was passed their way, and generally finding
enlightenment in the mad ride from girl to boy, from
debutante to queer, from California to Georgia that
Scott Turner Schofield navigated for them. And I, the
cynical live performance critic, sat among them,
sweet tea in hand, a fan in the making.

Scott, it should be said up front and often, is simply
a mesmerizing performer. You could listen to his
voice all night. He has comic timing tattooed on his
genes, and he can make the trip from irony to
sincerity in 3 seconds flat. Take a classic moment in
"Debutante Balls" when Scott has wandered in his
boy persona into a drug store looking for a make up
counter lady to transform him from boy to
debutante:

Desperate times call for desperate measures.
I approach the makeup counter. Betsy, a 79-
year old native South Carolinian greets me
with a smile.

"Hi there, son. What can I do for you today?"

I think, "Oh, Betsy. Fate has brought us
together. Will gender tear us apart?"

"Um, Ma'am, I need some makeup."

[Pause.]

"You do?"

"Yes Ma'am. You see, I'm a...I'm a woman."

Well, while the actor writhes in his predicament,
Betsy understands that action is needed, and she
reaches for the intercom button and announces:
"TRACEY, PLEASE COME TO THE MAKEUP COUNTER.
WE HAVE A SITUATION." Tracey is as bewildered as
Betsy, but both older women respond with a mixture
of improvisation and empathy. Needless to say, Scott
makes it to the dance on time, make up intact, ego
somewhat frayed, and gender in a state of flux. This
is just one of many moments in the opus of Scott
where hilarious snuggles up right next to poignant
and cliché sits happily next to deep dramatic
insight.

As Scott loves to say, you cannot make this stuff up,
or, more exactly, "credibility waits for no
performance artist." Tying truth to falsehood, gender
to performance, and all of the above to geography
and class, Scott is a prophet in motion. It would not
be quite right to call what he does a "one man
show," because like Peggy Shaw and Kate Bornstein
before him, Scott cannot limit himself to one man.
He moves through identities like a drag queen in a
medley or a femme in a shoe store. And as he twists
his lithe body in and out of dresses, T-shirts with
slogans, leopard print panties and boxers, the
audience gets to experience gender like a fun fair

ride—ups and downs, shocks and lulls, thrills and exhilaration. But this gender in motion is not an actor's gimmick for Scott nor is it prescriptive or a manifesto on fluidity. No, Scott's real argument is for complexity. In a utopian moment, he explains:

> At my Grand Gala Ball of Coming Out, everyone will be required to wear a white dress, or else tuxedo tails and nothing else. A kiddie pool of sweet tea will be the dance floor as we wrestle with our complex identities because we all, every one of us, are complex, slippery, and tasty. We'll dance to bad eighties music as we lick and suck the excesses of multiple oppressions off one another. We'll all come out for what we are, and see ourselves reflected in one another's body glitter.

Sounds incredible...unless, like me, you have an antipathy for coming out narratives, slippery genders, and eighties music. Not to mention body glitter. But one man's utopia is...well, one man's utopia. And that is Scott's point. His journey has brought him to this junction, and in his story, perfection comes in form of the complex, the slippery, and the tasty. And that's where Scott and I agree. No better place to begin than the complex, the slippery, and the tasty, even if my Grand Gala would not showcase eighties anything and may feature less communal licking!

But I digress. In a way, Scott makes a queer art of digression. The art of going off track, leaving the true way, exiting on the wrong ramp constitutes his theatrical signature. Every step of his transition on the road from youthful confusion to adult perplexity is a digression; and every digression is a smart, entertaining, complex, and funny narrative about sex, gender, and Krispy Kreme donuts. I know, it is weird, but Scott manages to turn the Krispy Kreme phenomenon into a metaphor for sex change. I will never see a donut the same way again, and I love donuts. Digression leads to new paths, roads uncharted, territories off the map and off the wall.

But always, Scott leads us back to the prom, the ball, the scene of queer adolescent humiliation that, in his capable hands, becomes an opportunity in retrospect for a new and different understanding of the rites and rituals of coming of age in heteronormative USA.

In between the tidbits of advice ("You've gotta know how to make an entrance—how to be gracious and take it in stride—if you want to survive,"), the deep questions ("Spit or Swallow?"), and the locker room insights ("Queer invisibility has privileges a straight boy would die for,") are nestled nuggets of personal revelation ("I inherited my grandfather's nipples somehow,") and challenges to received wisdom ("Oh I'm just begging for someone to steal MY identity.") Reading this short and precious book of scripts and essays could definitely rock your world, and if you are smart, you will sit down with a Dixie cup of sweet tea and let the rocking begin.

 *J. Halberstam is Professor of English and Gender Studies at USC. Halberstam teaches intro to gender studies along with other fun stuff and hopes that there might be other Scott Turner Schofield type geniuses out there in the lecture hall taking notes. Halberstam is known for her books* **Female Masculinity** *and* **In a Queer Time and Place: Transgender Bodies, Subcultural Lives** *and is finishing a book on alternative knowledge production. Halberstam is thinking about writing a book about bats next...weird, but true.*

underground transit
by Kt Kilborn

This show premiered at Charis Books and More in Atlanta, GA, in December 2001 and has seen over 50

productions since then, including: Vamp/Re-Vamp at The PushPush Theater; the Philadelphia Fringe Festival Fresh Fringe Series; the Southern Comfort Conference; Queer @ HERE: the Celebration of Queer Culture in New York City; sTaGes: New York's Transgender Theater Festival; and LadyFest South.

This solo was created with utmost gratitude for Peggy Shaw and Kate Bornstein. Thank you for showing me that there are no answers except, perhaps, in what you live in your body.

The show is dedicated to Marsha Johnson, Brandon Teena, and everybody else who has died for living.

SCENE I

[The performance space is set up like a subway car.
Audience members sit in seats that face each other
across an aisle, which is the stage. House lights stay on
throughout, lighting both the performer and the entire
audience. The performer, at this moment THE YOUNG
WOMAN, enters with the audience and takes a seat. She
is wearing the most feminine version of whatever is
fashionable: a skirt and tight T–shirt, for instance. She
carries a large backpack. She studies her subway map as
the audience settles. Sound can be controlled by a
technician or on a boom box that the performer brings
onstage. Train sounds rise, then fall. She turns to a
nearby passenger to begin.]

THE YOUNG WOMAN:

Would you believe I was almost Homecoming Queen
in high school?

Picture it:

Football field, fluorescent light.
Ms. Congeniality at my side,
Ms. Best Dressed next to her
and me.

Blank stares, nervous laughter.

I gotta tell you some things,
you gotta know where I'm coming from
to fully grasp the
nightmare
that was this night.

I didn't, like, get my period in the dress,
I didn't even trip on the field, which is good for me!

But when I was a boy,
and I was a boy
back then,
way back when...
When I was a boy,
I'd have given anything

for a girl
like I became.
Homecoming Queen?
Are you kidding me?
I dreamed about her at night
she was Donna,
and I was Ritchie Valens.
(Lou Diamond Phillips, Los Lobos
remember that movie?)

[Opening strains of Los Lobos' "La Bamba" play: Air
guitar solo! Music stops.]

But the controls that socialized me into
Homecoming Queen
were multifaceted.
But I'll get to that in a second.

My life as a boy included:
years with no shirt,
two decades (and counting)
of wrong bathroom incidents,
and more than a few phone calls home from school.

At eleven years old
I got a psychologist.
She told me:
No, I wasn't any kind of boy
and boy
did I need
a training bra.

I thought,
"Training for what?"

[Claps hands and falls down to do push–ups.]

I was seventeen years old
when got my first period,
a day late and a dollar short.
Did that make me a woman?

Make me a woman
make

me
a woman?

[Push–ups end. Slow rise.]

Or was it the years I spent after
growing my hair
and padding my bra
so that I could fit in
in a world of illusions
when I didn't even
fit
in my own body?

From readysetgo
with the training bra on
my world was training me
training me to be.
It's funny what a piece of clothing
will train you to see.

(And in between all of that,
what about sexuality?)

[Train sounds.]

Someone once asked me—
on a train like this,
in full, strange public—
"How long I'd been gay,"
whether I am "totally lesbian, or, you know,
just more bi than straight?"
And,
"If you're wearing the pants,
does that make you
the man?"

"Are you asking who I fuck
or who the fuck I think I am?"
I asked said concerned citizen.
Confused at the distinction,
this woman turned and ran.
Like, she got off the train!
I wanted to run after her,

I wanted to say,
"HEY LADY!
I'm sorry!
I'm not really all that hostile,
it's just a little more
complicated
than that!"

[Train sounds.]

Now I don't expect y'all to see what's inside of me.
You couldn't anyway, we're not trained that way,
To be sensitive.

I think it's some kind of defensive convention.
We're taught never ever to mention
anything a little
queer.

So of necessity
comes invention:
The girls who feel like boys
start to dress in a way that says
yes
to anyone looking through what we learned
about style and intention.

Me?
I went to New York
in between definitions.

A Southern dyke in my head
I went swimming in the East Village bar scene,
came out wondering
where the hell I had been
all along.

It's all about your hair
and what you wear!

I feel like I'm on the F,
Brooklyn bound,
the way it comes up from underground
into the light.

Sexuality and gender is one long soul train
in this town,
and all the girls are on board.

[Train sounds.]

So it's all about your hair
and what you wear.

Did you notice
I'm wearing a skirt today?
Found it in my closet,
balled up between some Tevas
and a pair of straight–legged Dickies,
under a bunch of wide silk shirts made for men.
I thought I'd try it on,
let the breeze flow with ease
between my legs.

[THE YOUNG WOMAN pulls out her NYC Transit
Authority map, unfolds it wide.]

I was checking my direction
on a map in Grand Central.
A short guy in a suit,
cute
but not my
type,
entered into the intimate zone of
my personal space,
asked me
which way I wanted to go.

I said,
"I just need to get from here to there."
He said,
"Baby, Girl,
I'd take you anywhere.
Why don't I give you my number,
and you can call me when you get yourself
safely home?"

He followed me to my platform like a dog chasing a
bone.

I turned around
I stared him down
I said
"Sure,
I'll give you my number."
Then, just to play, I heard myself say,
"That is,
that is if you like
boys
anyway."

Shocked, his jaw dropped.
"You're a—a—a...?"
"Sure."

He turned with nothing else to say,
turned on his Armani heel and walked away.
So I got on the train to ride it out,
went underground to talk about
what we never ever
talk about
on the street.

[Train sounds.]

SCENE II

[THE YOUNG WOMAN studies the map, changes seats.
She holds the map against herself, traces the red 1/9 line
from chest to groin.]

I once rode the 1 and 9 from Van Courtland Park
all the way
to South Ferry.
I don't know how many blocks that is,
it's just a dip under the river and a whole lot of time.

You don't sense much on that kind of ride,
maybe you don't even think "rapid" transit
should take that long.

I certainly never believed I could fall asleep
against the roar of the tracks,

though I'd seen a few Hassids roll their eyes back
behind their prayer books
on the ride home from work.

Man, I fell hard.
I'd been up all night
talking art
with a Chicana
who couldn't remember my name
when morning came.

When I felt the train scrape across the curve
of Manhattan Island,
down in the place where they tell everybody
to get the hell off,
y'all,
I jumped out of my dream—
I couldn't believe all I had seen
as I had arrowed
unconscious
through the heart of the city.

[THE YOUNG WOMAN leans in to tell this story.]

I dreamt that I woke up,
and here the weirdness began,
in the loft bed of the storeroom I rented on 1st Ave.

I was late!
I bolted from my bunk and shot down the ladder
turned on the taps as I emptied my bladder
put my fingers in the cool sink stream
that faded from rust–tinged to clean.

I got up from the pot
turned the taps on to hot
and splashed the water on my face.
I opened my eyes
and jumped back in fear
at what I had seen appeared
in the mirror.

My face.
Yes mine, but with
hair:

Stubble and a mustache.
The first thought to cross my mind?
Sure,
"Oh FUCK!" and "What the hell?"
But too:
"I don't have
a razor."
(As though, in the dream, I'd always had hair
but preferred that
this face
stay clean shaven.)
The thought of greeting the world with
this face
Don Johnson gone Chong
had me mortified.

I ransacked the room,
found shaving soap and a leg razor,
then fought with myself
who'd seemed to know, that
"You can't use a leg razor on the face."

I was pissed
I was late
but I couldn't stop staring,
I couldn't stop caring
about what They would think
when I walked out the door.
I saw the faces of my friends,
would they think:
"Poor, poor kid,
what a mess she's in now."
Would they run from the
man–girl freak show
I'd become?

As I spiraled through neurosis after
Seinfeld–would–envy–me neurosis,
the face calmed me down.

Didn't say a word
didn't move its lips
just stared into my eyes
(its eyes my eyes),
and she told me.

Right to the back of my soul
I heard him say,
"You know, maybe it's supposed to be this way."

[Train sounds.]

Then the grating of wheels with no axles to bend
on the curve of the island
even subway miners couldn't mend.
The screech and the racket woke me up once again.
Awake for real this time, right?

I shot up and stared at a mirror of glass:
The window lit up against the unending black
of the tunnel that took me from one end and back
of the city that saved me
the city that woke me
the city that took me for the ride of my life
through an infinity of girl
to one end of boy
and there,
alone
myself,
I sat.

SCENE III

Three Finger Cowboy's "Trouble Yum" (Daemon Records)
blasts through the car. As the song plays, THE YOUNG
WOMAN produces jeans and a white T-shirt from her
backpack.

She pulls down the skirt, revealing starched white boxers.
From under her tiny-T, she pulls a lacy bra, which she
aims at a passenger like a slingshot, and fires. She pulls
on the white T-shirt and the jeans, dancing to the song.
By the end of the last chorus, she has changed clothes
into her identity as the BABY BUTCH/BOY-DYKE, and
she stands at attention.]

"Oh lordy here she comes
That girl is trouble, yum.
Hang onto your pajamas

The girl is trouble, yum.
Do what you're going to
I only wanna rock with you.
I wanna rock with you!
Good heavens here she comes
the girl is trouble, yum
Go on and tell your mama
the girl is trouble, yum.
But don't wait for her
because you'll wait for the rest of your life
you're seeing double
oh that girl ain't nothing but trouble!
Here she comes
she's trouble, yum!
Here she comes
she's trouble, yum
Here she comes,
she's trouble, yum!
Oooooh yeah!"

BABY BUTCH/BOY–DYKE:

If Barbie set the standards for "drag queen" tastes,
then for grrrls like me, I say,
"James Dean never knew what a fashion statement
he was making."

You ever see yourself in some misplaced mirror
or on the reflective foundation of a skyscraper?
You're walking along to the music in your head
and you trip
when you see that reflection.
You trip
on how different you look from what you thought,
maybe just since you stepped out the door
maybe
your whole life.
You trip
maybe you stumble.

You wonder if the cats behind the glass
are getting a good laugh at you,
pulling on your skirt, or
scraping your hair down around your ears.

So, you move on,
holding on
to that image of you
projected for everyone to see
inside.

Inside of me I had a picture
my whole life
looked a lot like this,
until I learned that people
can be mirrors.
Until I saw my
self
reflected in the faces of strangers
as cold and alien as those structures downtown.

[Train sounds.]

Have you ever seen a train derail?
Ever been on the platform for too damn long
and, then there's folks walking single–file
along the glow–in–the–dark line
crying?

Whatever.

I was cruising through a summertime,
responsibilities on the line,
loved a girl who could make you
stand
whenever she entered the room.

Her parents invited me out to dinner.
Man, I felt like such a winner:
Winning smile, winning charm,
and this girl on my arm.
I went as I was.

I strutted up to the door,
wondering if there'd ever been a cat as cool as me:
Confident, assured,
just me.
Then she opened the door.

[A sweet song here, like Elvis' "Fools Rush In."]

Evening summer light warmed even more
as it molded to her body,
and the red dress she wore.

Come with me for a second.
Imagine
the most beautiful
red dress.
Then
the
most
incredible looking woman
you've
ever seen,
and she's wearing it.

Call her what you want,
call her a he if you need to,
but tonight
this woman
was with me.

But it seemed it wasn't
queer night
at the country club
this evening.

I dropped my forks.
I sloshed my wine.
I felt a mask
crust over me.

I'm too ugly
I'm too queer
to be with this red woman.
I couldn't laugh
I couldn't speak
I could only feel the way the room
looked at me
when we walked in the door.

I mean,
sure

it was my appearance,
but wasn't that my expression?
Wasn't my hair
and everything I'd thought to wear
the image of my
self
projected
for everyone to see?

She took me home
wouldn't let me walk alone.
The kiss goodnight
became a
"Spend the night?"
invitation.

Once in my room she looked at me,
said I hadn't been the gregarious girl
she knew me to be,
though I was
at least
the perfect nervous boyfriend.

I lowered my eyes
I started to cry
I told her everything:
The mask,
the thoughts I hear inside my head
that I imagine come from others
when faced with me and her,
the woman in red.
How,
in the context of what others see,
regardless of her love for me,
I see myself...
No, it's that I *can't* see...
I'm just not the boy
I want to be.

[Explosive:]

Why the roles?
Why the box?

Didn't butch/femme die
in a fiery wreck
twenty years ago
with all the rest that wasn't
mainstream, middle–class dreck?

I thought of the vision that came to visit me
that one late morning
dreaming beneath the city.
Maybe
I am
the way I'm supposed to be.

But sometimes I like to pretend I'm the ghost
of some fifties bull–dyke butch,
reborn in too feminine a body,
in a time too streamlined by what's correct
to live to be what I'd like to reflect.

"Sweetheart,"
she said,
and oh, how she put her hands on me
lowered her hot thighs onto mine,
"Baby, you're boy enough for me.
But I wouldn't be with you
if I didn't know just how much of a
woman
you really can be."

SCENE IV

[Train sounds rise again, then a song. The BABY
BUTCH/BOY–DYKE listens reflectively for a moment to
"Baby I'm a Star" by Three Finger Cowboy (Daemon
Records).

He pulls a compact mirror and a blue eye–liner pencil
from the backpack. He draws two blue tears coming from
his left eye, a star on his right cheek and returns the
compact back to the bag.

The music shifts from contemplative to rocking, and in
this moment, he jumps up from his seat, grabs the bag,

and opens it again. He pulls out blue pants, a blue shirt, and a studded belt. He takes off his costume, sometimes handing, sometimes chucking the pieces at the audience, and re–dresses to become the BLUE BOY by the end of the song.]

"Nobody really knows me
not so far
How could you ever own me?
Baby I'm a star
How could you hope to hold me?
Baby I'm a star,
yeah I'm a star.
I give you everything
so why can't you be happy for me?
How could you ever own me?
Baby I'm a star
How could you hope to hold me?
Baby I'm a star, yeah I'm a star.
(rock out)
How could you hope to hold me?
Baby I'm a star
How could you ever own me?
Baby I'm a star
Nobody really knows me
Baby I'm a star
Yeah I'm a star
I'm a
star
I'm a
star."

THE BLUE BOY:

The first time I rode the F train to Brooklyn,
I thought the tunnel was lined with mirrors.

[Train sounds.]

Sitting, staring out the dark windows
right around 2nd Avenue,
a string of faces cruised by,
first fast like a disco

then slow enough to make out eyes,
the nuances of smiles.
I thought I saw my face reflected back at me.
Then it hooked a right and went South
toward Grand Street.

I thought:
"Could that have been the boy
I left behind in childhood,
the guy I never thought I could be,
the face
that thought so hard at me,
and opened my gender–swollen eyes?"

The next time I rode the train to Brooklyn
I turned my back to the aisle.
I waited until we caught the BDQ again.

I saw him.

I knocked,
then pounded:
"Hey man! Hey!
Who are you?
What am I?
Where do we go?"

[Pause.]

What can I say?
It was 2 a.m. the full moon of a Friday.
My fellow passengers weren't too perturbed:
It was me against a guy whose fillings blasted
Snoop Dogg and Patsy Cline
on each alternate, open–mouthed chew
of a pork rind.

My guy the next train over never responded.
He just looked me up and down,
and with a furrowed brow,
turned away before the turn in the tracks.

So fucking much for duality.

[Train sounds.]

SCENE V

[The BLUE BOY, lost in thought, is suddenly called to attention by the backpack. He opens it again, discovers something that makes him smile, and pulls out a blue suit jacket. Sending a prayer of thanks to Mother Butch herself, Peggy Shaw, he slips into the jacket. He looks like deep running water in sharkskin.]

Sharp, isn't it?

When I bought this suit,
I asked the tailor
I said,
"Hey man, don't worry about offending me,
but,
do I look like a guy to you?"

He looked me up and down,
laughed a little,
then said,
"Oh Honey, not with those hips.
I'd still take you out."

Nah, no offense taken.

It's a damn fine suit, wouldn't you say?

I wore it one night with the woman in red,
and I was satisfied.

Except,
and this is the problem of the
feminist consciousness,
I woke up early the next morning,
my arm bridging the gap between the
curve of her hips
and the
swell of her breasts,
thinking.
I thought,
"The whole world still knows
how much of a woman I am,
even if I'm not wearing

'three pieces of clothing
to match my sex'"
as once was the law.

I had dreamed of Paula Martineau
and Georganna Lagen:
Two dykes imprisoned after the death
of Paula's young daughter.
It took their juries
seven years
to decide
that the death had been
an accident,
given the circumstances.

I wondered if Paula and Georganna looked any
softer
after all that time.

See, there's a sharpness to a lesbian.
I'm not decreeing, it's just what I've seen:
Right around the eyes,
it says,
"Fuck you.
I won't fit into the box you've made for me,
and if I must, my eyes will speak for me
across the checkout line,
on the porch of the house
with four kids."

I can't stand that sharpness.
It cuts me.
Paula and Georganna had it,
but nobody sees it in me without denial.

No, I am short–haired self–confidence!
I just haven't found the right guy!
I am a woman!
Confused!
Riding the night train through the Bronx
after all the kiosks have closed.

So when I awoke that dark morning,
my body pressed up against hers,
I realized that we're in a different

class,
Paula and Georganna and I.
If it's not about money,
then it's about
passing.

You be the judge:
on my day in court
would you put me away?

Girlish tits and hips that still look good
in a man's suit.
Would you put this queer away?

[Pauses, takes off jacket and gifts it to an audience
member. Turns, unbuttons and removes the shirt, then
turns again and pulls the T-shirt off to reveal the ACE
bandage that binds her breasts flat.]

What about this one?

[Train sounds.]

I never thought I would say
I am beautiful.
No, I am hard—edges and tattoos
I am fast cars and guitars
I am hard for her when it excites us
and so, so soft
to her touch.

[Seeing something in one audience member:]

Paula?

Paula, girl, I would write it on my body
in sticky black letters
on some hard wall of my body
for you
if it would make any difference.

If it would make anybody
see.

[Suddenly aware of his nakedness, the BLUE BOY grabs back his jacket and makes to run out of the playing space. As he pulls on the jacket, his hand catches on a card in the left inside breast pocket. He pulls it out, regards the figures displayed upon it. Then he shows it to the audience, saying:]

Have you seen my friend Brandon Teena?

Have you seen my friend Marsha Johnson?

[Moving quickly up the aisle, showing the card with photographs and birth and death dates to anybody who will look at them.]

Brandon Teena, Marsha Johnson!
Hey! Hey, have you seen my friend?

SCENE VI

[Train sounds blend into a meaningful pop song like The Cure's "Boys Don't Cry." THE BLUE BOY opens the backpack once again. He pulls out yet more costume pieces, then stops to take off the jacket and the pants. Handing those around to the audience, he pulls down the boxer shorts, revealing a pair of leopard print panties. He pulls on the T-shirt he has just removed from the bag. It reads "Smart–Ass Whiteboy." He pulls on oversized yellow skateboarding shorts, then futzes with his hair as he dons a matching yellow visor. While all of this is happening, he speaks the words of the song as though it is a private conversation to a lost lover or friend. Boyishly androgynous, waiting to break expectations, s/he broods until the end of the song.]

Wasssuuuuupp??

'Till I was eleven years old
I thought I was a boy.
Could I have turned into this?

Look at what we do to our boys in our culture.
Does this boy look like he's got a

feminist consciousness,
like he's got a thought worth much of anything
rolling around in this head?
I mean, does this
yellow
say "smart and articulate"
to you?

Like I said,
the controls that socialized me
into Homecoming Queen
were multi–faceted.

Yeah, but it's a whiteboy's world, right?
We let them go, and we don't
face the consequences.

If I'm oppressive, you're repressed!
Oppressive, repressed
repressive, oppressed
If you're repressive, I'm oppressed!
Oppressive, repressed
repressive, oppressed...

It doesn't make any difference.

It's not about your hair or what you wear
or what you got going on down there.

As long as we are standing
at the door to the law,
we're letting the folks behind it
control everything.

[Falls down on the floor to do push–ups.]

Yeah, I wore that training bra,
I went through the decathlon of puberty
training me
training me
training me to be
a woman.

[Stands up to do jumping jacks.]

I'm with Ani DiFranco. She said,
"You could try to train me like a pet
You could try to teach me to behave
But I'll tell you, if I haven't learned it yet,
I ain't gonna sit, I ain't gonna stay."

But maybe I don't wanna be a man.
Maybe I like it just fine, thank you,
exactly the way I am.

Man, like this, I got choices.
I can elect myself
King of the World!
Or be selected by my high school peers as
Queen for a Day.
I want an identity card for this moment,
you know what I'm saying?

It's not about your hair
or what you wear.
We are bodies in a metal tube
hurtling fast through time and space
gender and race.
We're all the same way down here on the subway
we're sweating on each other!
So what are we gonna do to get there?

Where?

[Train sounds.]

There.

Where the space inside lives out loud,
where social control goes underground,
and we can speak with our mouths full
of who we are.

[Moving amongst the audience, clasping their hands.]

Who am I?
Touch me.
What am I?

See me.
Where am I?
Taste the air with all of your most beautiful senses,
and then:
Tell me.

Without saying
a word.

[Amy Ray's "Mtns of Glory" blasts (Daemon Records).
S/he yells to the audience: "Throw my clothes back at
me!"

Juggling with the shower of trousers, T–shirts, and
underpants, s/he changes through the series of costumes
s/he has worn throughout the show, turning the gestures
s/he has used to play each gender over onto themselves.

S/he unwraps her/his breasts, then covers his/herself with
a jacket. S/he retrieves a tiara from the bag, puts it on,
then reaches into the bag again, and pulls out the
rainbow–colored silk dress from that fateful October night
and dances with it to the beat of the song.

"Call up my rockboy finally score
He's got drama like a toreador and
Me and the bottle we're on the mend
I'm tired of winning gonna lose again
I said I'm gonna miss being the boy
I'm gonna miss being the man yeah
I'm gonna miss being the boy
I'm gonna miss being the man yeah
When I go down to F L A
Sand in my shoes think of you
I can't get it out it's kinda rough
I like the way it feels but it's not enough
I said I'm gonna miss being the boy
I'm gonna miss being the man yeah
I'm gonna miss being the boy
I'm gonna miss being the man yeah
I said hey baby don't you need me now
Mtns of glory
Mtns of glory
I said now hey baby don't you want to feel these

Mtns of glory
Mtns of glory
I said hey honey don't you miss me now
Mtns of glory
Mtns of glory
I said hey honey don't you want to feel these
Mtns of glory
Mtns of glory
I'm gonna miss being the boy
I'm gonna miss being the man yeah
I'm gonna miss being the boy
I'm gonna miss being the man yeah
I said I'm gonna miss being the boy
I'm gonna miss being the man
I'm said hey baby don't you miss me now
Mtns of glory
Mtns of glory
Yeah"

[As the last screech of the song fades out, s/he stands,
clothed in everything, and asks:]

Would you believe I was almost
Homecoming Queen
in high school?

The End
(for now)

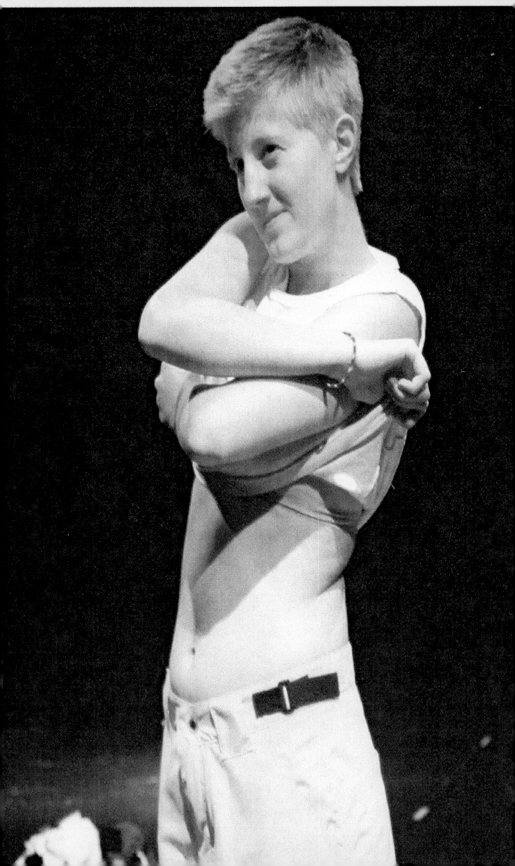

Debutante Balls
by Scott Turner Schofield

An early kernel of this work was presented at SEEN+HEARD: Atlanta's Celebration of Women Artists. The first full script premiered at the Chicago Single File Festival in 2004. In 2006 the script was significantly revised, and the show was directed by Steve Bailey, presented with support from the National Performance Network, at Jump–Start Performance Company in San Antonio, Texas.

The show has received more than 30 presentations, at such venues as FRESH MEAT (part of the National Queer Arts Festival), Trans/Giving in Los Angeles, and the Fresh Fruit Festival in New York City.

This show is dedicated to Holly Hughes and Carmelita Tropicana, and the debs: Elizabeth Asti, E. Keller Barnhardt, and Carson Efird, for their early encouragement, and for the examples they set of how to be the woman you are, or emphatically are not; and to Tim Miller, for the booster shot of performance courage that made this solo complete.

"[C]oming out is not, fundamentally, a confession, even though it often takes that form; and its ultimate purpose is not to help anyone understand. Coming out is a discipline of reclaiming ourselves from oblivion by getting rid of the fears that cut us off from who we are."
– Michael Joseph Cross

[Audience members enter a chamber of light and propriety, having been graciously handed a small Dixie cup along with their crisp program notes. Johann Sebastian Bach's "Air on a G–String" plays softly. The stage that greets them displays the white dress of the Debutante atop a short runway platform. Easily mistaken for a wedding dress, it glows on its rack, lit from behind so that each pearl and embroidered white flower stands out. The performer, SCOTT TURNER SCHOFIELD, hides inside the many layers of tulle that make the bell of this belle.

In the audience, two ushers hold two pitchers of sweet tea. There must be enough sweet tea for everyone. Another pitcher of sweet tea sits behind the dress onstage.

Once "Air on a G–String" has reached its climax, TURNER, wearing his screen–printed tuxedo T–shirt, tux pants, and red tennis shoes, throws open the bell of the dress and begins.]

SCENE I

TURNER:

I only did this Debutante thing so that I could get inside a debutante's dress.

[TURNER disappears inside the dress again, then slowly rises up behind it.]

Do you ever feel completely out of place? Like, so wrong in the moment that you feel CAUGHT...

[TURNER gets trapped behind the dress in the spotlight.]

as though the cops are coming, and they've got their spotlight trained on you, and you could run and run, but that bright light's fixed on you so you glow—like a cat's eye—no matter how far you run from the scene of the crime, the scene of yourself?

You've gotta know how to make an entrance—how to be gracious and take it in stride—if you want to survive.

Sometimes it's smarter to stand in your truth, act innocent, like: "Sure, that light's on me, but why shouldn't it be? And why don't you have a light, too?"

[The spotlight fades out. TURNER pushes the dress completely aside, addresses the next lines to it.]

When I first asked another Southerner how she enjoyed her Debutante Ball...

[A startling, you've–got–it–wrong alarm sounds.]

She rolled her eyes and drawled,

"Wrong class, Honey. Hell, wrong dyke."

How the hell was I supposed to know? That wasn't my experience—one way or another, all my friends came out. But you can't go mixing metaphors, I understand. I'll try to do better.

[Sinking inside the dress, playing hand–puppets underneath the skirt.]

It's possible you have no idea what I'm talking about. Debutante Balls? Doesn't that mean fancy parties and lady things? What's that got to do with being transgender? With coming out?

[TURNER disappears again, reemerges between skirts of tulle as though veiled. "Air on a G–String" plays softly.]

For those of you who may not know, and there are many—Yankees, transplants, and Southern–born alike—the Debutante Ball is a rite of passage for the elite. Young women and their families in the highest social circles still refer to the seasonal process of entering society as a marriageable woman of good manners as coming out. Coming out, in this context, is like Homecoming on steroids—Prom on acid.

["Air on a G–String" cuts out.]

Depending on your city, your state, your social circle, you could come out at sixteen, eighteen, or twenty–one years old. You pray to get a summertime Gala or face making your debut in a long white dress after Labor Day!

[Alarm sounds.]

Isn't that what coming out is all about anyway?

I know I said I wouldn't mix metaphors, but no matter who you are—when, where, why, or how you come out—you are always just a girl, standing in a spotlight, awaiting acceptance in a long white dress, long after Labor Day.

[The spotlight beams high.]

You gotta know how to make an entrance, how to be gracious and take it in stride, if you want to survive.

[Lights fade back to the warm general wash.]

I should know: I am a three–time debutante! Well anyway, I've come out three times. The only thing I never did was wear that long white dress and bow, gracefully, to Society.

But you know, this performance is a gala event! And I'm not coming out of here until we all acknowledge that.

Acknowledgment is the key: When I came out as a lesbian at sixteen years old, nobody acted any kind of surprised. Not a soul responded as though my bold statement of queer identity deserved a single cork pop of celebration! There were no bows, no applause... Y'all, I am a performance artist today because of that overwhelming disappointment!

The Debutantes understand. Coming out should be your own made–for–TV–movie–of–the–week, the kind that ends in a Ball with the date you've always wanted. I'll take it further. I always take it further. I think that we all deserve a Grand Gala—or, if you prefer, GAYla—Ball, when we come out! It's that difficult, it's that important to come out as whatever it is you are.

Alas, I digress. This will happen a lot tonight.

So tonight, this is a Gala Celebration! We have light, sound, this beautiful dress; you have me to accept, and I have you to accept me—of course, you're the audience—that's your job!

Right?

[Pause. Alarm sounds.]

Fine. Well, first I have to come out. You have to clap. Okay?

[The spotlight turns on as the audience hopefully begins to clap. There's an applause track on the cue CD to augment it, or make it funny—whichever works.]

Okay then. I'll come out.

[TURNER steps through the dress and out of the dress rack. He curtsies in the long, foot–sliding, chest–parallel–to–the–floor way of the Debutante.]

I am so honored that y'all have attended this Gala Ball of Coming Out. Truly! That's not just the lip service of Southern hospitality. I am so honored, that today I made y'all...

[TURNER produces a pitcher, lit by the spotlight, filled to the brim.]

a nice big pitcher of sweet tea. I set it out on my porch especially! I blended it with light from the sun, then filled it with sugar so sweet you'll think you could catch diabetes from it.

[TURNER walks out into the house to pour sweet tea in each audience member's Dixie cup. At some point, he must return to the stage. USHERS take up the gracious tea pouring so nobody feels left out.]

They're Dixie cups! Get it?

Now, I realize that some of you might have some problems drinking out of Dixie cups. But don't imagine I don't know what I'm doing.

[Pause.]

See, here's the thing about the South, the South where I live: Where I live in the South, we understand ourselves as somehow complicit in the history of our region, where James Baldwin called "the scene of the crime."

We roll our eyes when we talk about where we're from. We say "Atlanta" and "Charlotte" and "The Woodlands, Texas" out of the side of our mouths, like it's a drink we don't like, but have to swallow.

I feel the same way when I talk about being white. White gets real particular when you modify it with Southern. Or so everybody would have you believe.

[Pause.]

Did y'all know that restaurants in Georgia can be fined for not offering sweet tea? "It's the house wine of the South," don't you know. I'm not sure what that has to do with whiteness... Except that it seems to be everywhere, like a good glass of sweet tea in Georgia, and I can't get the taste out of my mouth.

[Pause.]

When I travel, I ask for sweet tea, and seven times out of twelve I'll get some fruit–flavored swill or else it's just understood that *that's* what the sugar packets are for.

When you're in Georgia, they don't even ask which way you want it—you want sweet until you ask otherwise—and there's a special system of spoons and lemons for un–sweet tea drinkers, just to let everybody know.

[Pause.]

I don't have to come out as white—the whitest, most neon–white person you may ever meet—but whiteness is the backdrop... No! It's the sweet tea, served without question, to my story.

(I do have to come out, and tell y'all that I am sick of the way white stories are assumed the most palatable. I just want to be given another choice—a thousand more choices—in my movies, my TV shows, my heartfelt performances about coming out; and I don't want to feel like I'm ordering off the menu.)

Since I'm in the mood to come out, and since I don't have a spoon or lemons to change the flavor, I thought I'd offer my whiteness to you sweet. You may drink it up or leave it untouched—it wouldn't be impolite.

And it brings us to an eternal question, one which affects all of us, the Debutante perhaps most especially:

"Spit or swallow?"

It's the swallowing of tradition when you're untraditional yourself that's so interesting to me. I never knew a debutante in my generation who did this thing for herself. Coming out, for these women, is just a big party to please the parents or grandparents.

(Privilege does weird things to context, doesn't it?)

But, how much do we swallow? How much can we take?

[TURNER drinks down most of the sweet tea. Hopefully someone will start a keg–stand count.]

How far can we spit?

See, so often we sit silent in the face of tradition when all we want to do is take our clothes off and scream and run into the dark night of making things new.

Right?

[The spotlight shines on TURNER.]

But it's *difficult*, complicated, so often times we don't. But no matter what we say—or choose not to reveal—there's always that spotlight marking you different. You feel it on your skin, your cheekbones glare, and you can't close your eyes against it. So, you stand still, act innocent, and look for that light in the people around you so that you can survive; until, at some point, you are swallowed whole.

[TURNER falls slowly out of the spotlight into darkness, where he also hides the pitcher.]

Or else you spit yourself out.

[Propelling back into the spotlight, of his own accord.]

But sometimes, sometimes there's just no other way to go about it but to step into that spotlight and take a bow; because you know what they say, don't you? It's not so much coming out, as it is coming through.

[Lights return to warm wash.]

SCENE II

Well anyway, I said there was a story about debutantes, so a story I will tell.

[The opening strains of something appropriate for the timeframe and identity, like maybe k.d. Lang's "Summer Fling," plays. TURNER prances around the stage, straightening the gorgeous white dress to the "Bat–dat–dad–ut–dahs."]

It's the summer of 1997, and my best friend Elizabeth Asti is coming out, too. She's not queer, she's a debutante, but don't think the two are mutually exclusive now! "The path across the ballroom floor is far from straight."

Liz had to spend her summer attending parties: Meeting people so she could come out into Charlotte society.

That's it! That's all it takes: "Hello, how are you? May I have this dance?" A curtsy here, a handshake there, a drink and a cigar at the open bar... Do that once for every debutante all in the same summer, throw a big fancy party at the end, and *voilà*: You are a member of Society.

But me? I wasn't Elizabeth's attendant in coming out like we told my mother. I had other kinds of coming out to attend to. My first Debutante Ball was the perfect cover. My debutante friend became my alibi.

The summer of Elizabeth Asti's Debutante Ball was my hot, sticky summer of love. While Liz donned white kid gloves in one hundred percent humidity and sipped sweet tea at one of her deb season's twenty–four parties before the grand Coming Out Ball, I stayed up all night to watch streetlights glow in halos of humidity and saw the road, after the rain, run like a river of fog before the first light of dawn dried it back to asphalt.

I was in love. With her.

[That alarm sounds again.]

No, not Elizabeth Asti! Though, like I said, I always wanted to get in a debutante's dress. But I'm getting ahead of myself there. While Liz met every socialite in the city of Charlotte, County of Mecklenburg, Queen City of the South, I got my earlobes licked, my thighs stroked, my shape molded by Abby Lowe.

Abby Lowe came from the wrong side of the tracks. In Charlotte, North Carolina, this means you live in the shadows of the big buildings. It means that the sun shines flat on your side of town while the south–facing First Union building glitters on the Bank of America, then shines on the Wachovia, casting a warm glow over Providence Road and the rich side of town.

I'm not sure if they planned that. It wouldn't be polite to speculate.

But I loved Abby Lowe, and I wasn't about to let any one way street system or Friday night road block get in the way of my first love.

[Pause.]

I think I'm going to digress again. Am I? Yes.

What was a nice girl like me, who lived on the light side of town, doing with a dyke like Abby Lowe? How did I get away with it? Didn't I have parents? I hear you asking.

I have written papers, editorials, *manifestas* about queer youth invisibility. About how the world is so sexist and heterosexist that it relegates the real life of queer people to the margins. Half–inch margins. Written in white ink on white paper. Which in itself is problematic. But you know what, thinking back, invisibility had its perks:

"Mom, I'm going out with the girls!"
"Mom, there won't be any boys at the party!"
"Mom, she's a debutante. Sleeping in the same bed means nothing to her."
And so, the saga of Abby Lowe.

[Pause.]

You remember how I complained, graciously of course, that I never got my own Gayla Ball of Coming Out? That summer of Elizabeth Asti's Debutante Ball, I did get a moment in the light.

Now, I could paint a picture of a South that does exist. I could relate horror stories of family estrangement by community arrangement and describe the loneliness, the sometimes despair, the oftentimes danger of growing up queer in the South. I could tell those stories, and those stories would be true. But in my South, even in Charlotte, which we called The Anti–Queen City when I was coming out, there was a place for a queer kid like me to go and just be.

If you were a queer or questioning teenager and you could get yourself out of your house and down to Time Out Youth's church basement, you could be all of yourself, if only for an hour or two on Mondays. And that coming out meant everything. It meant existing in your own life, loving in your own right. It meant visibility, legibility, and some kind of common language that told you you were not, in fact, the crazy, godless heathen your church billboard told you you were. (It isn't possible to overstate the facts there. It's what I know from coming through.)

My weekly visits to the visionary queer youth support group even meant meeting a nice girl like Abby Lowe over Diet Coke and sugar cookies! So I had that going for me. I had a place to go and a place to say I was going, even if they weren't exactly the same place.

One day during that summer of coming out all over, we all sat down: A crew of black sissies and softball playing tomboys, white boys missing football practice to come out, and poor girls who wore their femininity like an impenetrable shield of mascara, shiny nails, and perfect hair. We complained, not so graciously, about the fact that we couldn't go to any Gay Pride Parade in case our parents saw us on TV, and we didn't go to Prom—the Teenage Coming Out

Ball—because we couldn't go with the person we wanted. And so...we made our own.

I used every Debutante Gala planning day possible for my Gayla Ball. Elizabeth, the debutante–alibi, had me working like a dog!

"Mom, how do you rent champagne flutes? Yes, Mom, that is a mirrorball in my car. They need it for the...Afterparty. Hey! Could I borrow your ABBA CD?"

Other kids do drugs. You know?

The Gayla Ball happened in the middle of July. You didn't have to wear a tux, you just had to come as you were or as the wildest imagination you had of the person you might some day become. Ezekial wore the bra they tore off him at school, and Tamara gave him her feather boa to cover the broken straps. Martin, the other fag from my high school, bought me this T–shirt, and he wore the rainbow scarf I sported the night I almost got elected Homecoming Queen. Abby dressed herself as femininely as her soon–to–be–enlisted–could–do–more–push–ups–one–handed–than–I–could–do–on–my–knees frame would allow; and we elected Ezekial Prom Queen and Abby the King, and after the dancing was done, we all piled into a rented limousine and drove out to the Jesse Helms Senatorial Library in Wingate, North Carolina, where we danced on the lawn like the crazy, godless heathens our dear, faithful Senator told us we were.

[Something ironic and disco, like maybe Ike and Tina's "Disco Inferno" blasts. It cuts out as the spotlight catches TURNER in mid–disco dance groove.]

Can y'all please imagine for a moment the scene when the Wingate Police arrived?

Ezekial had his tongue down Tommy's throat, and my hips had Abby's handprints all over them when the spotlight came on. We didn't know what to do, we didn't know what to say, when the cop hollered from his car:

"You know, I don't think y'all are supposed to be doin' that."

What did he mean? I mean:

"Which part?"

[The spotlight fades out to warm lights of love about to bloom.]

Before we let go that night and had to go home—to the part–selves we lived at home—Abby invited me over. You know what THIS means! Now here's where the digression feeds back into the real story.

SCENE III

I called my mom from Abby's apartment. I told her,

[TURNER recites the following in his sweetest Southern girl accent:]

The Sanderson's Debutante Pool Party ran late and that I'd be staying with Elizabeth, whose house I was calling from, since she was so close by and since we hadn't finished folding Bird of Paradise napkins for the Mother–Daughter Tea that Liz and her mom were to host the next day.

I said I'd come home early from Liz's house, where I was calling from, so Mom and I could get ready together, and we'd finally go together to a party where she could meet all the people whose elbows I'd rubbed all summer long.

My mom sounded wary when we said goodbye, but what did I care, right?

The next morning I drove home across town, my windshield glaring so badly in the cross–town war of sunshine and reflection that I had to stop at the Athens Diner, an All–Nite working class joint on the north–west corner of south–east Charlotte (where kids like me ate to feel authentic), to have some coffee and rub the light out of my eyes.

Y'all didn't think I was gonna kiss and tell, now, did you?

When I got home, I crept into the kitchen to take the back stairs to my room. There, at the table, sleeping, sat my mother, a Bird of Paradise folded in front of her, and a box of unfolded napkins at her feet.

Oh, shit.

I kept creeping quietly past my fast asleep mother but of course the one loose floorboard you always try to avoid...

[The alarm sounds, as loud as you might imagine it would in this situation.]

Mom wakes up! The allegations fly! Liz's mom came by to drop off the napkins I was to fold and bring to the Tea, and what's WORSE—and I know this is unbelievable, it's just that credibility waits for no performance artist—we got Caller ID the day before, only I didn't know, because I was at the Gayla Ball! Mom knew Liz's number by heart and what's more, she knew that the prefix 864 meant I was calling from the wrong side of the tracks.

Did I mention that Abby got kicked out of her home at seventeen for being queer and now, at nineteen to my sixteen, lived in her very own apartment, all by herself, on the wrong side of the tracks?

Picture my mother awake in the early summer morning staring at her kid wearing...

[Indicates the costume. The spotlight shines hard.]

I was about to go from teenage lesbian invisibility to a big queer splotch of smudged mascara on the face of the straightness she expected of me.

[The spotlight cuts out.]

But we're not there yet—no—my mother: My five-foot-three, white-ass British mother sitting in her Laura Ashley BREAKFAST NOOK on the South side of Charlotte, North Carolina, asks me, quite seriously:

"Have you been...smoking crack?"

Much later, a friend of my mother's would tell me that Mom would have preferred I play into her media-made, racist worst nightmare instead of the one I made real for her that morning. But I just had my Gayla Ball, and I didn't need any sweet tea. I swallowed hard and said,

[Here the spotlight beams again.]

"I'm not a drug addict, Mom! I'm gay, don't you get it?!"

Then I grabbed the napkins and ran out into the street, the hot Southern summer street of making things new.

[Out with the spotlight, out onto the street.]

Clearly, that part of the story is over, but there's just one last piece to tell:

I headed back to the Athens Diner and folded the napkins on the table.

[TURNER takes up a tail of tulle from the dress.]

It would be nicely theatrical to fold one of these fuckers for you, but they take three minutes apiece for my clumsy hands, and back then I had 127 to fold! Finally I folded them all, and I took off because I was late to the first of two parties I was actually expected to attend all summer long.

I hit the Mint Museum, of which the Asti family had rented a wing, 15 minutes late for the party—excuse me—the Tea. I have no clothes to change into, but I believe I can pull this off if I act ironic enough. (I didn't know, then, that when re–inscribing tradition, Southerners, well, rich people generally, don't appreciate irony.) I spend the next ten minutes traipsing the back halls of the museum, trying to find a door to the Tea. I don't know how I found it, and I don't know how I didn't see the EMERGENCY EXIT ALARM WILL SOUND sign.

I walk in late, without my mother, my arms laden with Bird of Paradise napkins...

[TURNER pushes the dress, which has become this door, and it clatters down on the platform. A different alarm sounds: This one is long, continuous, and loud. A fire alarm. He tries to behave, as she did back then, that it was not happening...]

and make my entrance into Charlotte Society.

SCENE IV

Social dust settles. It flies, but it settles. The next year I went off to college and started studying women. Women are *fascinating.*

I came out a Feminist during my first year of college and, by some lucky twist of performance art fate, my debutante ties remained intact. I found an invitation in my dorm mailbox (the one with the radical feminist fist stickered to it) informing me that:

The Debutante Guild
of Charlotte–Mecklenburg
delights in inviting
me
to a Gala Debutante Ball.

My recently–radical blood quickened in my newly feminist body as I imagined the possibilities: "Think Globally," they say. "Act Locally."

[The spotlight beams loud and proud. TURNER's speech sounds like fiery feminist spoken word.]

I started thinking up ways to inject feminist rhetoric into polite conversation. I imagined I would make my entrance, saunter down the receiving line of gracious hostesses, give them the secret handshake of radical feminism, and soon we'd all be doing an electric slide of liberation! We would tear down the interlocking systems of class, race, gender, and creed that built these Balls—and why do they gotta be called *balls*, anyway? And it would be as easy as tearing crepe paper streamers off of those grand mahogany staircases.

[The spotlight fades out, like the fire in TURNER's young activist soul.]

When I left college, I lost a measure of my feminism. Let's say my radicalism lost momentum. Not everything is fuel for my fire anymore, and this is good, because going to somebody else's party and telling them what's wrong with it, point by point— well it ain't classy, and it is far from gracious.

So we're not gonna talk much about my behavior at my second Debutante Ball, if you will permit me that discretion. We'll say I made a smudge mark on the card of proper social decorum and left people thinking, "Ain't that just like a *feminist*."

What I've figured out is: Nobody stops a party in the middle of the fun. The party only stops when nobody shows up. Yes, the Debutante Ball is a celebration of a system of secret handshakes most people will never learn. It is also Society's tea to spit or swallow.

But it's not that I've lost my radicalism, and it's not that I'm not still a feminist. I can still imagine, hope, and work for change.

At my Grand Gala Ball of Coming Out, everyone will be required to wear a white dress or else tuxedo tails and nothing else. A kiddie pool of sweet tea will be the dance floor as we wrestle with our complex identities because we all, every one of us, are complex, slippery, and tasty. We'll dance to bad eighties music as we lick and suck the excesses of multiple oppressions off one another. We'll all come out for what we are and see ourselves reflected in one another's body glitter.

[Pauses to contemplate it all.]

You'd think that by now I would have had that party, but no. Just goes to show, those debs have huge balls, coming out the way they do.

I'll explain:

I have come out more times than should be allowed. First I was a lesbian, then I was a feminist, then I was transgender, now I'm a transsexual...

That's a whole lot of transitioning. Too much to describe all in one sentence, but...I think we're about ready for another digression. Yes?

Dance with me.

[The sexy intro to a tango plays.]

When you learn how to dance, I mean dance like a debutante, you learn how to move in a box made of a man's arms. You learn exactly where to put your feet on footprints already set out for you across the ballroom floor.

I learned to dance on the feet of my fathers, tapping out the rhythms on the tops of their shoes. When I learned to dance on the feet of my fathers, I didn't think of it as following: I was learning how to lead. I learned a different kind of dance some years later in the darkness of a dyke bar, grooving to a beat I liked better. But the music never quite felt like my own.

Then I hit the ground.

While the traffic of straight and gay moved around me—on different days, in different directions—I stepped out of the two–step grooves, treading on toes and bumping shoulders as I made my own way.

Coming out trans felt like catching the ground. Learning a dance all my own, learning that a dance *could* be my own, and that a dance works best when two bodies that know themselves move, and catch each other in the groove.

[A chorus from something fun to dance to, like maybe Billy Idol's "Dancin' with Myself" plays loud. TURNER grabs people from the audience for a dance party moment! If he could get the rights to do so, he would sing along to the part about having nothing to lose and nothing to prove, and then the song would fade, and the dancers would return to their seats with a round of applause.]

So—we're all clear on that?

Good.

Now let's get back to how the debutantes do it.

I love the way that debutantes come out: Throw a party! Invite your friends! Dance your ass off and come out as you are.

I can acknowledge that it's difficult. There are issues of ethnicity, community, citizenship, belonging, of wanting to belong to any group that will have you. So maybe I'm making this sound easier than it is.

But maybe...maybe I haven't told y'all the whole truth. Maybe it's time to confess, myself. Stand fully in my truth. See how it feels.

[TURNER ducks behind the dress. Blackout, then he lights up a flashlight inside the the dress, He becomes lit like a shadow puppet.]

I'm not so sure why it's so hard to come out like this. I come out all the time. I make a profession out of coming out. But I do have a secret. In fact, everybody has this secret, but it's a *secret*, so we never talk about it. I want to tell you, I do, but, oh, what are you going to think of me??? Will you still love me tomorrow?

[Pause.]

Dammit, here goes! I'm coming out!

[The spotlight fires up, then comically falls slowly to the bottom of the skirt, where all that has come out is TURNER's head.]

I'M...I'M...I'm middle class.

Yes, that's right. I'm not a real debutante. I mean, they say *nouveau riche* is better than no *riche* at all, but I didn't even have that. Only nobody knew any better, because it wasn't polite to ask. Sure, they hadn't seen me at middle school cotillion classes. Their families hadn't known my family since they all swooped in and started oppressing people. But we all went to private school together and got cars on our sixteenth birthdays and went to Debutante Balls in the summer, so I was some kind of an insider, right?

In the mid–to–late–nineties, middle–of–the–road middle class could mean all of those things! Standing on your tiptoes and on top of your parents' two mortgages and a maxed–out credit card, you could see the inside of the upper upper upper upper upper upper upper "middle class," just so long as you were white and had some manners and no cars up on blocks in your front yard.

I know. It's...embarrassing. I'm supposed to be so much more radical than this. I passed for rich all the way through high school, and I pass for radical almost everywhere I go these days. But here I am...revealed.

I see why some people opt out of coming out. This is awkward.

But no, I gotta keep going. I have to set an example:

[TURNER propels out of the dress.]

I do things like...drive my dad's Crown Victoria while drinking Perrier and blasting hip–hop, and I think I'm cool while I do it! I would rather put a down–payment on a house than get sex reassignment surgery the day (and I'm confident it will come) when I suddenly have enough money to choose.

So on the one hand I'm a radical, but I'm bourgeois middle class, and, on the other hand, I'm an aristocrat, but I'm bourgeois middle class. Is it possible that being bourgeois middle class is really just like being transgender, minus all the pronoun confusion and gay panic fear? Stay with me here:

When you can't tell a person's gender identity or their class status, it is never polite to ask, and class status, like gender identity, is something we discern by what we display or don't. We all know rich kids who go thrift store shopping, right? (That one got a huge laugh at Vassar...)

And when you're a male–identified queer who likes to sleep with brilliant women, are you a radical sexual renegade or just a straight assimilationist, when all you're trying to do is be you?

I'm tired of me. I want to know about you.

[At this, all lights black out and TURNER retrieves the flashlight. First, he shines it on himself.]

I call this game Coming Out COPS Style. Me? I'm a closet karaoke rockstar.

[TURNER then scans the audience, stopping randomly to ask the lit–up face to come out as whatever feels important to them. There's a plant out there to lead us into the next bit, but if someone looks particularly uncomfortable coming out on the spot like that, TURNER graciously asks: "Do you think you may be NORMAL?" At this buzzword, TURNER turns the flashlight back on himself.]

NORMAL?

Now normal, normal is its own identity entirely. "Normal" people complain that at least I have a label. That I, the feminist, transgender, pre– and perhaps never–operative performance artist, have it easy. All of my identities have a place to go: a support group on Monday nights, a Pride parade in June, or a March on Washington in April in which to feel that I belong. Normal people must fight their battles alone, face their fears and calm their doubts in the lonely closets of their normalcy.

Okay, so I have it easy. It's me and the Debutantes. But what if normal people would come out, too?

There'd be a place for nose pickers to go, a support group for the chronically tardy, a Pride Parade in April for the Sunday afternoon window shoppers, and a March on Washington in June for everyone who masturbates or swears to God they don't. You know who you are.

The legions of normal people must come out, like the Debutantes and the Queers, to be known for the normal people we all really are. Imagine how much better you'd feel, standing in that spotlight, accepting that applause.

[Lights go out as that applause track returns. TURNER shines the flashlight back on all the brave or crazy audience members who just came out.]

It feels good, right?

SCENE V

At the time of my third Debutante Ball, I was
21 years old and far from normal.

My friend, the deb—a lesbian (at the time)—called
me up and begged me to support her through the
classism, the racism, the stifling heterosexuality of
her entrance into high society.

"You just can't wear a tux, will you promise you
won't? I mean, I understand your identity these
days, and you know I fully and totally support you,
you sweet lil' transman you, it's just that
everybody's going to have known you since you
were seventeen on the Homecoming Court, and my
grandmother's already on oxygen, and..."

"Pish–tosh!" I say. I'm not very offended that I can't
come costumed in the gender that is my own. I can
be as queer as a three–dollar bill in a dress, right?
But what kind of dress does the transgender,
feminist, pre– and perhaps never–operative
performance artist I've become think to wear to
make his entrance into the silk wallpapered halls of
High Society?

I only own one dress.

[TURNER produces his party dress. A long black satin
skirt boasts a leopard print bustier.]

There are rich people in my life who would have
gladly shelled out if they thought Vera Wang was
just the injection of femininity I needed to become a
nice society girl. But no! I wore this dress to two
Debutante Balls before. Doesn't matter that it's been
three years, three inches in height, and three full
identities: Third time's a charm! So I take my dress
and my high heels and head out to Greenville, South
Carolina.

[Pause.]

I get to Greenville, and I realize that I just don't know what to do with my hair. I'm in the habit of telling any hair stylist that there's no moment in my life where I ever need to look feminine. Ever. It's how I invite SuperCuts into transgender tolerance. But that's another story. In Greenville, where they say, "The higher the hair, the closer to God," I wished I hadn't been so adamant.

I had imagined that I would arrive at the 5–Star hotel (of which a room had been pre–paid for me!) to find a gaggle of half–dressed girls fighting for mirror space, applying mascara, blow–drying hair. These girls never mind helping out their ignorant–to–the–ways–of–*Seventeen–Magazine* fellow Ball–goers. You pretend that you are illiterate to the lexicon of liquid eyeliner and lipstick, and at some point you'll have dozens of finely–manicured, feminine hands touching you all over: rubbing eye shadow on your eyelids, spritzing and fritzing and futzing with your hair. This has happened to me before. Queer invisibility has privileges a straight boy would *die* for.

But, when I arrive at the 5–Star hotel, the snooty concierge informs me that: "The ladies have all gone to the salon."

[Oh, that spotlight again....]

I would have to make *myself* look *pretty?*

[Out it goes. Timing is everything.]

It's not that concierges, as a race, are all snooty assholes. It's possible this guy was being snooty because he didn't like the way I looked. I was not the dapper individual you see before you here, no, when I arrived at the 5–Star Hotel, I looked like this:

[TURNER dons a bright yellow visor and T–shirt that reads: "Dirty Gay Frat Boy."]

Which leads me to another very important question: What is it about queers and slogan T–shirts?

I mean, straight people wear slogan tees, but somehow they're just not as clever, or succinct.

Now, just to be clear here, I refer to "straight people" as anyone who is heterosexually–oriented and traditionally–gendered. Which, if you knew me, you'd know I am. Sort of. I refer to "queer people" as anyone who would make George W. Bush uncomfortable, and we all know that's a lot of straight people.

Now, you'd think that since heterosexuality is everywhere, you'd think that people would say funnier things about it. You'd think that since the traditionally–gendered get to wear themselves on their sleeves with relative impunity, you'd think that someone would create some kind of wash–n–wear humor for those identity politics. Not so, my friends.

I conducted an exhaustive Internet search, Googling terms like "straight humor"+"T–shirts" (in toggle quotes), and all I could come up with was…

[Peels off frat boy shirt and the tuxedo tee to reveal one reading "RUNS WITH SCISSORS."]

Is there a straight person in here who can explain this to me? Is there a straight person in here?

Even feminists are funny when it comes to T–shirts!

[Reveals "EVE WAS FRAMED" T–shirt.]

But still, queers have the market.

[TURNER takes off one shirt after another: A "T" shirt from the National Center for Transgender Equality, "I CAN'T EVEN THINK STRAIGHT," ending with a slogan that reads "TEN PERCENT IS NOT ENOUGH—RECRUIT! RECRUIT! RECRUIT!"]

But forget the concierge! How am I going to fix my hair? What will I do with my face? I run from the 5–Star hotel onto the Greenville, South Carolina street, and there, on the corner, shining like a great neon red–and–white cathedral in the sunset, stands a CVS!

I am saved.

[Handel's "Hallelujah" chorus blasts for a moment as TURNER prances across the stage ecstatically.]

SCENE VI

I walk into the CVS in Greenville, South Carolina, and the first thing I hear is:

"How are you today, son? What can I help you find?"

I think to myself: "This may be a problem" and make my way to the magazine rack, where I comb every copy for tips and tricks, but Cosmo only wants to tell me about The Best Orgasm I'll Ever Have, not about how to apply liquid eyeliner or whether blue eye shadow's really still a faux–pas (it just goes so well with my skin tone). I call every femme I know, but today's the day no lipstick lesbian or transsexual will answer her cell phone.

Desperate times call for desperate measures. I approach the makeup counter. Betsy, a 79–year old native South Carolinian, greets me with a smile.

"Hi there, son. What can I do for you today?"

I think, "Oh, Betsy. Fate has brought us together. Will gender tear us apart?"

"Um, Ma'am, I need some makeup."

[Pause.]

"You do?"

"Yes Ma'am. You see, I'm a...I'm a woman."

[Pause.]

"You are?

[Pause.]

"You ARE!"

"Yes, Ma'am, it's a long story, but right now I'm going to a Debutante Ball. In less than three hours. In a dress."

Betsy reaches under the makeup counter. I start to think she's pushing the EMERGENCY CALL THE COPS button, but no, she pulls out a white telephone, and over the loudspeaker in the CVS in Greenville, South Carolina, I hear:

[Over the loudspeaker, as TURNER gets locked once again in the spotlight:]

"Tracey, please come to the makeup counter. We have a situation."

[The spotlight fades out, along with the blood in TURNER's face.]

I could not make this up even if I wanted to. After what feels like thirty years of standing rooted to the spot, Tracey arrives. Betsy, bless her heart, fills her in:

"This is a woman."

[Long pause.]

"Oh my God, it is!"

"And she is going to the Debutante Ball in less than three hours in a dress."

[Long pause.]

"Oh my God, you are?"

I begin to have one of those out–of–body experiences so common to transpeople. I think to myself: "What the hell kind of class warrior have I become? These women are working well past retirement age, no doubt to fill emptying social security and Medicare coffers, and here I am, this queer, white, class–passing queer, asking them to help me go to a Debutante Ball?!"

I return to my body. Tracey is eying me. She looks me over for a moment, then smiles, and says,

"Well, what color is your dress now, Babygirl?"

I am so overwhelmed by the genuine warmth in her voice that I hardly even hear myself say: "My dress? It's leopard print."

SCENE VII

[Scene VII is all action. Something ironic, playful and Southern, like maybe Johnny Cash's "A Boy Named Sue," plays as TURNER strips down from the tuxedo outfit, puts on makeup, and sprays glitter into his short hair. Then he puts on the party dress—feet first, like pants. He takes off his shirt to reveal her breasts, bound with an ACE bandage. Maybe he says, "What? Like it's any more extreme than this," indicating a Wonderbra, which he fires like a slingshot into the audience. He puts on the dress (he keeps his BVDs on) and asks someone to zip her up. Tries to cover up his armpit hair, his tattoo, the fact that the dress will only zip halfway up his back, and picks up a shawl instead to cover it all. Puts on the shoes. Stumbles around in the chunky three–inch heeled shoes. Remembers the BVDs, strips them off to reveal leopard–print panties. Finally, he's ready. She looks much better than you might think. A perfect curtsy finishes it off.]

SCENE VIII

[In the spotlight, TURNER–in–a–dress says:]

Do you ever feel out of place? Like so wrong in the
moment that it's as though you're caught, and the
cops are coming, and they've got their spotlight
trained on you, and you could run and run but you
can't hide because you glow—like a cat's eye—no
matter how far or fast you run from the scene of the
crime, the scene of yourself?

[Pause.]

So, I got an invitation to the Great Gala Debutante
Ball of Greenville, South Carolina. It told me the
date, it told me whom I would be honoring, but the
only address listed was: The Assembly. There's a
particular kind of privilege that comes with
debutante ties: It's like every place belongs to you,
even places in South Carolina that you don't have an
address to. I got there anyway. Once he saw me
looking like this, the concierge helped me out.

But when I arrive at the undisclosed location, the
white man at the door won't let my ass in. It seems
that I am not accompanied by the requisite male
escort, and furthermore, my gloves are not the
correct length.

[TURNER indicates with the glove, leaving it two inches
below and then stretching it two inches above the elbow:
"Acceptable—Not Acceptable." "Debutante—Harlot."
Clearly.]

I wait outside until finally my debutante party
arrives. There are live violins and a red carpet, and I
swear my friend's dad is just going to pop all of his
shirt studs with pride. He escorts in his debutante
daughter, then waltzes back for her debutante
mother, then foxtrots over for his debutante mother.
Finally, they roll up the red carpet, the dudes with
the musical instruments disperse, and he comes
back for me. He's like a Boy Scout, hustling the

socially–challenged across the red carpet of High Society.

Before my critiques start to become self–righteous, I make for the open bar to drink myself into feeling comfortable in my high heels.

[TURNER finds the pitcher again and his own Dixie cup. He begins pouring shots of sweet tea for himself, downing them as he speaks.]

I know that when people say,

"Oh, I like your hair. Bet you don't have to do a thing to it!"

[Takes a shot.]

and, "Leopard print! Now I couldn't pull *that* off!"

[Takes a shot.]

that they're not being nice, not really, but what do I care. I've got a gin and tonic number...

[Takes a shot to cover the actual number.]

and glitter spray in my hair!

Through the fog of gin, tonic, cigar smoke, and Laura Ashley, a woman approaches. She's the parent of a friend of mine from high school. Normally, when I meet parents of friends of mine from high school, I tell them I do something respectable to make them feel better about the job market and how much money they spent on our educations. But this time, I'm drunk. I tell her the truth. I tell her:

"I'm a performance artist...

[The Spotlight fades up as TURNER's speech devolves drunkenly:]

I do work about gender and sexuality. My gender and sexuality, spezzzifically. I'm transgender. What's that? Oh—no, Ma'am, I was not born with a penis. No, um, do you know the difference between gender and sex? Oh don't worry! Most people don't! It's a great place to start!

[Takes a shot.]

Okay. Okayokayokayokay. Sex! Sex is what you're born with, and gender! Gender's what you do with it. Right? No.

[Takes a shot.]

You can be anything you want, SEX IS NOT DESTINY! Only most people won't tell you that. Most people don't even know they could be something different, most people don't have the words to tell themselves. And you have to tell yourself. You have to learn a vocab–vocabab– vocabulrly. Words. You have to learn the words to figure yourself out, the right words to tell yourself and the world. Y'nowhadimean? Y'nowhadimean? Y'nowhadimean?"

[TURNER snaps out of the drunkenness.]

This woman raises one eyebrow, leans right in.

"You know, I work with a woman, her name's Michelle, but she used to be Michael! Can you tell me how that happened?"

["Air on a G–String" fades up, holds softly through the next speech.]

Once again, I could not make this up.

You gotta know how to make an entrance, how to be graceful, and take it in stride, if you want to survive. If you want to describe sex reassignment surgery in all it's gory penis–to–vagina, or vagina–to–penis, and breasts or no–breasts glory.

If you want to explain the difference between transsexual and transgender, and how transvestite is complex, too; what it felt like to be born a baby girl, but to grow up thinking you're a boy; to go through puberty and become, against your will, your mother's only daughter. How this is so much more common than you think, until this parent of your friend takes you warmly by the arm, walks you around the dance floor, around white girls twirling in long, white dresses. She says she thinks she understands, but there's so much more she wants to know, and the next time she sees that Michelle, she's gonna take that woman out to lunch, Honey. And that she is so glad you came, came out to this Ball in Greenville, South Carolina.

[Quiet, just for this line.]

Hey, you gotta know how to make an entrance.

[Lights fade. Something like the *Queer as Folk* rendition of Harvey Fierstein's "I Am What I Am" could play. Spotlight up on TURNER one last time as he lip–synchs the first verse, which is about wanting to have a little pride in your world, which is not a place you have to hide in. It's a delightfully–embodied female–to–male–to–masculine female drag sequence.]

FIN.

Becoming a Man in 127 EASY Steps
by Scott Turner Schofield

This show was commissioned by the Pat Graney
Company in Seattle, Washington; 7 Stages in
Atlanta, Georgia; and DiverseWorks in Houston,
Texas. It was made possible in part by the National
Performance Network's Creation Fund. Major
contributors of the National Performance Network
include the Doris Duke Charitable Foundation, Ford
Foundation, the National Endowment for the Arts (a
federal agency), Altria, and the Nathan Cummings
Foundation. NPN is a group of cultural organizers
and artists facilitating the practice and public
experience of the performing arts in the United
States. NPN serves artists, arts organizers, and a
broad range of audiences and communities across
the country through commissions, residencies,
culture–centered community projects, and other
artistic activities. For more information, go to
www.npnweb.org.

In 2007 the script was workshopped at the
Playwrights' Center in Minneapolis, Minnesota,
under the care of Hayley Finn and Deborah Stein.
The show was further workshopped at The
Evergreen State College in Olympia, Washington,
and its fledgling technical and design elements were
generously collaborated upon by Matt Lawrence,
Jeremy Reynolds, Dennis Mobbs, and several
committed students. It premiered at the Capitol Hill
Arts Center in Seattle, Washington, on October 26,
2007. Direction and lighting design by Steve Bailey
with dramaturgy by Kate Bornstein.

Thanks to S. Bear Bergman for the title, and to T
Cooper, Felicia Luna Lemus, and Joe Meno for their
decoding genius.

This solo is dedicated to my Mom, and the other women in my life who helped me become the man I am.

[Audience enters the performance space, where seating rises three–quarters around a very intimate floor–level stage. A long, blood red fabric hangs in the center, a sac knotted in the middle, where hides SCOTT TURNER SCHOFIELD, the performer. A mattress has been installed below this acrobatics tissu, and over it lies several random couch cushions and pillows. Lengths of white fabric drape from the ceiling, tucked in between the mattress and the floor; they will construct the audience fort. Clothes lines stretch around the outside edge of the seating, and a sheet hangs on the upstage wall, where images and video will be projected. Blackout, then fetal loop: Sonogram images light the fabric and the sheet. In voice–over:]

PRELUDE

[V.O.:]

Doctors wonder, want to know exactly what makes a person transgender. They hypothesize a rush of hormones at the wrong time, brought on by stress perhaps. I believe it is sheer will.

Yes, embryonic me imagined life infinitely more interesting as a trade between soul and body. And so, here I am.

[TURNER's body becomes visible in the tissu sac for the first time. He wears something monotone and neutral and tight. He is not bound or packing. He spends the remainder of the voice–over twisting, climbing, and falling, suspended in the tissu.]

I was not born in the wrong body.

[TURNER plays with, in, and on the tissu, pushing and falling headfirst, as if out of a birth canal.]

My father fooled around with a 19–year–old woman at a crucial moment in my fetal development. My mother caught them in the middle of it, wrapped around one another like baby twins. Call it a rush of blood to her head: I bathed in the trickledown of emotions when she kicked him out.

After their breakup, my father broke into the family storage space filled with the treasures he and my mother had saved for their new life as parents, for the time when they could afford to move out of their trailer and into a house together. My mother had taken their money for me, and so he took an ax to all of their things, smashing furniture, slashing sun dresses, shredding photographs—cutting their shared possessions in half.

Imagine embryo me, inside my mother, walking into that chaos.

Can you feel the hurricane flood of betrayal over love, hot anger and deep sadness rushing in torrents of estrogen, testosterone, and progesterone over baby me, cleaving gender from sex, body from self. There was no room for another man in my mother's life, only me. I could not escape this cascade of confusion, so I swam as best as I knew how.

Trauma or no, I would have been trans no matter what body I'd been born with. Drama or no, inside the womb or out, I am my own life. Mistakes are better understood as lessons to learn. Girl in boy's body or boy inside a girl, call it fate or biology, will or spiritual choice.

[On the floor, grounded, says:]

I was not born in the wrong body.

[Lighting shift: Warm and bright.]

ACT I

Remember when you were a kid, and making forts was the funnest–ever thing to do with your time?

I could make palaces out of couch cushions. Give me a sheet, forget about it, you'd have the Taj Mahal in your living room. I was a four–year–old Frank Lloyd Wright, all form and function. Hide me in plain sight, give me comfort inside an impressive facade. I would build and tuck and bind and build and then lay there spent, enjoying the darkness, all that room for the secrets of myself.

But that was just the problem. Myself, I was a hyperactive child with Attention Deficit Disorder long before doctors started throwing Ritalin around like piñata candy. I wanted perfection! Which, of course, was impossible to achieve; but with the assistance of others...

So, this is what we're going to do. We're going to build a fort together. I need your help.

[TURNER enlists the audience to help him assemble the fort correctly, pulling panels of white fabric to the back of the seating risers and attaching them with clothespins to the clotheslines. He asks two audience members to hold the opposite ends of the tissu, instructing them, with secret signals, when to let it drop. Finally, it's "right."]

What's that thing they say? "Nothing worth it is ever easy." The satisfaction of a well–built fort is indescribable.

[TURNER builds a fort on stage out of the couch cushions, crawls into it, and lies face–up to admire this fine group collaboration.]

See the way it drapes, the way it covers us from God and parents and the outside world? We can be ourselves in here. We can tell secrets that no one else will hear.

[V.O.:]

Hey Turner it's Sheri again. I just had to share this with you: The boys and I are at Krispy Kreme. We're getting some hot fresh donuts before Royce's haircutting brunch in the morning. So we were watching the hot donuts move through on the conveyor belt and get their sugar glaze on top, and Tendal said, "Mom look, look! It looks like they're being changed! It looks like they're being changed forever! Just like Turner!" I bet you've never been compared to a hot, fresh Krispy Kreme donut, but now you have. Bye!

[TURNER finds a graffiti marker and writes on a huge piece of cardboard: "No Girls Allowed." He looks at himself, looks at the women in the audience. Crosses out Girls. Writes in "Boys." Looks at himself, looks at the men in the audience. Crosses out Boys. Writes in "Lies." Laughs. This is performance art! Crosses out Lies. Writes in "Secrets" Then he pins the cardboard to the sheet with more clothespins.]

[Spoken:]

Y'all wanna know some secrets?

[TURNER pulls out a silver dollar from the crease in a cushion.]

Heads or Tails?

[If Heads, TURNER strips off his top, then speaks the appropriate text, marking himself with pink lipstick. When he's done with the first, he goes on to the second. As this is happening, a projection of a LETTER FROM A PSYCHOLOGIST shines, the words marking his body.]

[Projected:]

September 14, 2005

Dear Medical Professional,

I am writing this letter in strong support of Scott Turner Schofield and his desire to seek medical treatment with you. I am a clinical psychologist in private practice, and I have known Turner since July 2003.

Turner presents with a diagnosis of Gender Identity Disorder (302.85). He meets all necessary criteria for this disorder including: a) a strong persistent cross–gender identification (not merely a desire for any perceived cultural advantages of being the other sex), b) consistent discomfort with his (female) sex and a sense of inappropriateness in the gender role of that sex, c) no evidence of a concurrent physical intersex condition, and d) clinically significant distress or impairment in social, occupational, and other areas of functioning.

Our therapeutic work together has focused on exploring the impact of this GID diagnosis and the associated anxiety and depression that result from not being perceived correctly by other people. Turner has been very conscientious during this process and has explored all of his options for coping with the mismatch of his gender with the culturally available roles. He has been aware of his male gender identity since childhood and has identified as a transgendered person since becoming aware of this phenomena early in college. For the first year of our work together, he was hesitant to live fully in the male role, wanting to first fully explore the ramifications of doing this on his identity and relationships. However, he decided to change his name legally and to begin using the male pronoun in all interpersonal contexts in approximately March 2004, and this change has had a profound positive impact on his self–esteem and mood symptoms and has much improved his interpersonal and occupational functioning.

After living in the male gender role for over a year, Turner is certain that this is the appropriate role for him, and he would like his physical body to match his identity. Most importantly at this time, Turner would like his appearance to be consistent with his gender so that he can more easily move in unfamiliar social situations without awkward reactions to his male gender role or the need to continually explain himself to strangers. For this reason, he is seeking consultation with you regarding medical treatment options. I fully support this decision. I know that at this time, Turner seeks hormonal treatment and not surgery, and I support this choice. I also want to document however, that if he and his doctor were to decide that surgery or any other medical intervention were indicated, I would wholly support this as well. Turner has excellent judgment and is fully capable of making these treatment decisions for himself. I also have the utmost confidence that he will be compliant with medical treatment and that he will consult with me as needed regarding any emotional stress that this treatment may bring. I am excited for Turner as he takes this step, and I expect it to lead to a continuation of the gains he has already made since I have known him.

Please feel free to contact me if you have any questions or if I can be of any further help with this.

Heads:

If I had bigger breasts, what they'd do is cut me here and here. Then they'd reach inside and pull out the tissue and stitch me up, leaving scars, and I'd be very sternly instructed not to exercise or lift or do anything strenuous for a long, long time. Except I am a guy, so I would, and it would hurt, and I would have big scars. As I am a flat–chested female–bodied person, they'd make little holes *here* and *here*, put in a tube and suck out the excess, and again I would take a vacation from lifting anything, or wouldn't, and it would heal funny. And then there are the drainage tubes. They suck out the water that builds up in your body while you're healing, and it makes me faint to look at them. Then the doctor literally pulls them out, and you have to heal from that, too. Now apparently men's nipples are located just a couple of ribs above women's, but look at these. I inherited my grandfather's nipples somehow, so I don't think people will look at mine and think female. However, a lot of people get nipple reconstruction, where they cut it off, shave it down, and graft it back on. For a minute it looks a little like a pepperoni, and you pray you don't wake up with your nipple on your bedsheets. It happens! After six months to a year, all the swelling finally goes down, and you can start the day by throwing on a shirt and end it by sitting on your porch shirtless in the sun. And doing what you want with your body, that's what matters.

[If Tails, TURNER strips off his pants to reveal his vulva, then again with the lipstick marks:]

Tails:

There are many ways to let it all hang out. A metoidioplasty cuts the tendon holding the clitoris up against the body and makes it fall forward, creating the appearance of externally-hanging genitalia. You can have silicone balls implanted in your labia to make a scrotum—and I think about those hi-bounce balls you used to make in science class, and I always wonder, "Is that what they look like?" Probably not, but we should look it up. Now, if I wanted a penis, I'd need to have a phalloplasty. Here they take a muscle from your calf and the skin from your wrist. They take a nerve from your arm, too, and attach it to your clitoris so you can feel the whole thing. But first they graft the whole package of muscle, skin, and nerves to your stomach, and over a period of months or years and dozens of operations, they move it down to your pubis *here,* and then they attach it to your leg *here,* which looks a little like a luggage handle, but only until the blood starts flowing, and then they cut the connection, and finally it hangs out. You can even get an erection, either by sticking rods in the hole or by squeezing little pumps in your balls – and how much fun is that? And it's all insanely expensive, did I mention? So it's unfair to think of people as real men only when they have penises because that would mean only rich men—or socialist dudes—get to be real. And anyway I looked up this website called erectionphotos.com, where dudes send in pictures of their real penises so they don't feel so oppressed by the porn industry, and I found penises that are as big as my clit—which is huge, right? Say yes!—and even penises that invert until they get erect, and I finally got wise to the statistical reality that size just does not matter.

[When he's done, TURNER takes the neutral clothing and tries to wipe the lipstick off. He only succeeds in smearing pink gunk all over himself. He shrugs and puts on an outfit consisting of khaki pants, a button-down shirt, and a baseball cap from the University of South Carolina, which reads "COCKS" in garnet letters. As he changes, the following voicemail message sounds:]

[V.O.:]

Hey Turner it's Topher! I love your sexy voice, it kinda makes me hot, and I have to remember you're a straight boy. Hi! I've missed you. And I've been meaning to call you because Chris Johnson has been on the T shots for a little while now, and I'm wondering how long this "second puberty" thing lasts, because I kinda wanna kill him, because it's kinda like living with a seventh–grade boy. But it's also very entertaining. He smells like Clearasil all the time again. It's funny as hell.

[Spoken:]

Really, appearance is all that matters. When I look like this...

[Without the hat,]

people think:
Gay boy. Or teenager.

When I look like this...

[With the hat, bill facing forward,]

people think:
Straight boy. Or teenager.

And when I look like this...

[With the hat, bill facing backward,]

people think:
Lesbian.

People can make any story if you give them the right elements.

[TURNER chucks the hat into the audience, then rummages through the couch cushions and returns with a toy box. The box contains a number of elements: objects such as a smooth rock, condoms, a Ken doll, a pocket watch, matches, baseball cards, etc., with which TURNER will use to tell the stories with during the show.]

Alright, so, just for tonight, whatever I give you signifies something deeply personal about who you are. And yes, this is a commentary on the arbitrary associations of identity. It's my fort, I said so.

[He hands the objects around, noting particularly interesting ones in funny ways. The last object in the box is a decoder ring.]

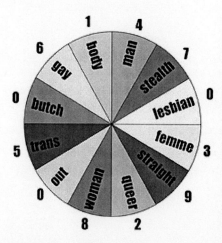

Sometimes I think it would be really useful to bring back the decoder ring, make it a part of daily life.

[The decoder ring, which is also printed on programs, appears on the screen. It looks like a pie chart, slices individually marked by such labels as "Gay," "Male," "Passing," "Heterosexual," etc. These words correspond to numbers, running 0 through 9 around the edge of the ring.]

If you see a person wearing a dress who's seven feet tall with an Adam's apple, you know there's a story there. How much nicer would it be for someone to take those visual cues, align them against a nonjudgmental scale, and say, "Hey, give me story number 53," rather than "What the fuck are you, freak?"

Every step you took to be sitting here with me tonight has a story: Maybe you shaved, or didn't. Perhaps you sat down to pee, or didn't—but in which bathroom? Of course, when you label all of these steps and parts of you, they don't quite add up to the whole, but if they did we wouldn't have drama and if we didn't have drama we wouldn't have any reason to MySpace, now would we?

Let's call out a number according to what you see in me—say, 127. Why 127? Well, it's prime and kind of a complicated mouthful, like me, and it's part of my social security number, which says EVERYTHING about my identity, apparently. Oh I'm just begging for someone to steal MY identity, you could get...

[The numbers 1, 2, and 7 correspond to stealth, queer, and body.]

Your very own stealth queer body! Or any number of other things. So now it's your turn. What do you see? What story would you like to hear? They almost never match up, what you see and what you get, but we'll have a good time getting there.

[The story section begins. As numbers are called out, TURNER finds the corresponding prop from the elements he has handed out to the audience.]

STORY SECTION 1.

[The following stories were told on the night of the premier. Others get told every night this show is performed. New stories will be posted at Homofactus Press, www.homofactuspress.com]

1. Get Fierce Hair

[Prop: Hair mousse.]

Hair is key to transformation, anybody can agree on that. Let's take a little trip down memory lane shall we?

[A slideshow begins, showcasing TURNER's hair through the ages. Something ironic and about hair, like maybe Amanda Lapore's "My Hair Looks Fierce" plays.]

I've had the same haircut for nearly 10 years. When people perceived me as a woman, they would say things like:

"Well I guess you have a quick morning routine."
and
"You know, that hair just says CONFIDENCE!"

[TURNER skooshes some mousse into his hand and begins styling.]

The only compliment I have ever received on my hair as a man went like this:

"Wow. The hair on your head is as soft as the hair on my balls was when I was 13. How do you do that?"

A new tagline for Pantene?

2. Learn to Dance

[Prop: Pink bow tie.]

I was awakened rudely into girlhood by Minnie Mouse. It was 1984.

One semester at afterschool daycare, the activity was tap dancing. To most children, the prospect of performing is terrifying. We already know how I felt. I had just seen Prince in his *Purple Rain* tour. I envisioned spotlights, purple smoke, Sheila E. grinding on stage and me keeping the beat to "Let's Go Crazy" in tap sneakers.

The tune we learned was much more tame: "Mickey Mouse's Birthday Party" played over and over again as we shuffle–step–step–turned on the classroom linoleum. There was one other boy in the class. So, in deference to symmetry, I believed I would play Mickey Number 2. I shuffle–turn–ball–changed at my end of the line, keeping an eye on the boy stage left. We both moved like robots, stumbling on the half–beats as the little girls added hip shakes and jazz hands to the routine. Everybody knows that boys can't dance as well as girls (except boys who danced better than the girls, but they went to real dance class or therapy, after school). So the other boy and I were quite clearly the two Mickeys.

The day of the recital, we arrived at the hall, and I saw my mother pull out a pair of white tights.

[TURNER dons the pink bow tie.]

I knew that Mickey Mouse did not wear tights, this was just the kind of shit my mom was always pulling, giving me lacy ankle socks and making me wear pink and telling me, "No, boys do this too." No wonder I turned out the way I did. As I balled up the tights, planning to run to the restroom and lose them in the trashcan, she pulled out patent leather Mary Janes affixed with my taps. Then a red skirt. Minnie Mouse?

[A picture of TURNER–as–Minnie is projected. The child looks cute with a little tail and floppy ears, but the eyes reveal the shame and anger within.]

3. Get a Tattoo

[Object: Fake tattoo.]

[TURNER brings someone on stage. He tells them that this is just between them. If the person has a tattoo they want to show and tell, they may do so. Then TURNER affixes each of them with one half of a fake tattoo. The tattoo is a replica of Picasso's *Matador*. The audience member chooses whether to be the matador or the bull.]

I want you to accept my skin.
I've been tattooing memories there,
and my body is a quilt I would wrap you in
as though you were a guest in my home.
I want to tell you with touch:
This is what's been done to me,
and this is what I'm doing with it.

I want to know where you're headed,
and where feels like home
in the breath we share between us.

[Exit audience member.]

4. Getting Your Rocks Off

[Object: The smooth white rock from Croatia.]

You know how you do things you wouldn't normally
do when you're out of your cultural context? I
wouldn't believe this story myself if I hadn't been
there.

At a theater festival in Pula, Croatia, I made friends
with my local technician and his bartender buddy.
We closed down the bar at 4 in the morning, getting
lit on Croatian Honey Schnapps, and burnt, too.
Petar, the bartender, all amped from his shift, insists
that I enjoy the salty waters of his country's
coastline without the bother of the tourists.

[A picture of the moonlit beach is projected on the sheet.
TURNER makes a beach out of the cushions and pillows.]

We had the stone cove all to ourselves. Go ahead
and send around that stone I took from that place,
whoever has it, so you can all feel the smooth and
cool underfoot.

Petar says, "Let's go skinny dipping!" and Atzo pulls
off his jeans in agreement, and when they're about
to dive in they yell, "What you do? Why not come
in?"

What am I supposed to say? Ah, well, this whole time you've thought I was a guy like you, when really I'm a transsexual, but I didn't know how to say that in Croatian. No. What I say is: "I, I have this thing. With my chest. I look...I look like I have breasts."

"What?"

"Breasts. Tits!"

They think this is a male self–consciousness thing. Plenty of guys have boobs!

"Do not be shame! This is Croatia, this is the sea, it is too beautiful. Come in!"

So I take off my shirt, but leave on my pants, and dive in.

[TURNER dives into the pillows.]

It's like bathwater, you know, when you sit and sweat and read and maybe jerk off, and then it's all cool and satisfying on your skin? It's gorgeous, the whole scene, but we are still three young guys together, drunk off our asses and out of our minds.

"All that could be better would be a girl, no Petar?" says Atzo. Petar's a partier, so he takes right off:

"Yeah! A girl we could fuck, she would love it!"

"Yes, here, in the water, we could all fuck!"

I...go along with it. I'm freaked out a little, scared of what could happen if we keep talking this way; all it would take is one drunken grab to the crotch and there I'd be, the resident vagina...but...I'm fascinated. I want to see if it's really true, what I've heard about guys making objects of women. When else will I get this chance?

In our defense I will say it was assumed the woman of our dreams would be consenting and enjoying herself, even if we were under thirty and two–thirds a virgin.

"But Atzo, you can't fuck a woman in the water," I say.

"Why no?"

"It is the water. The wet of the water, it stops the girl from getting wet. Not so good."

"What you are talking about? You don't need wet!" Petar cries, revealing his ineptitude and/or virginity. To appease my inner feminist after the filthy escalation of fantasy fucking, I tell the guys some secrets of the female anatomy, while also securing my place as a straight guy who has "fucked."

Then I notice they're...moving. Humping the rocks as I talk, sliding over and over on the cool slick stones that have warmed as we lay at the water's edge of the moonlit shore. Faster and faster and then I think, "Oh my god, this is one of those homosexual experiences they say every guy has, and this is definitely the gayest thing I've every been a part of but it's not GAY gay...and then..."

[Exhales loudly.]

Next story?

5. Chug

[Prop: Beer Can.]

[All action: TURNER chugs a beer.]

6. Be. Or not.

[Object: Soft Pack, held in a paper bag that reads "Surprise for a Boy!" TURNER pulls the flaccid silicone penis out of the bag and inspects it, a la Yorick.]

To be, or not to be: that is the question:
Whether 'tis nobler in the mind to suffer
The slings and arrows of outrageous fortune,

[TURNER slips the soft pack into his underwear.]

Or to take arms against a sea of troubles,
And by opposing end them?

One too many directors told me, "I can't cast you as a man because I know you're not really a man, and that just messes up my whole vision of the whole play."

Because directors, they are so visionary.

And so...I changed my identity again, changed my name, got a new headshot, and went out into the world as an actor. A male actor. Nothing more, nothing less.

To die: to sleep;
No more; and by a sleep to say we end
The heart-ache and the thousand natural shocks
That flesh is heir to, 'tis a consummation
Devoutly to be wish'd.

And there I was in the edgy gay theater in town, auditioning for an edgy gay play. It was the audition of my life! I was simply some young gay guy auditioning for the part of another young gay guy, because that's what acting is, and I was acting up a storm! The director loved me I could tell, because at the end of our 10 minutes, he tells me:

"I think this role was written for you. You're perfect. I want you. But I have a few questions to ask you—they are yes or no answers, okay?"

Okay, I say.

"Great. I'm not going to assume anything about your identity here, but, would you play gay, for pay?"

I'm comfortable with that. Totally.

"Wonderful. And are you comfortable with nudity?"

Absolutely. But what kind?

"I need you to do a full–frontal gay sex scene. Could you handle that?"

To die, to sleep;
To sleep: perchance to dream: ay, there's the rub;
For in that sleep of death what dreams may come
When we have shuffled off that mortal coil
Must give us pause.

"Ah, I see I've made you feel uncomfortable."

Oh no! I'm not uncomfortable. It's possible you're going to be. See, I'm an actor, I can act whatever part you believe I can. And I am very, very comfortable with nudity. I just can't be naked and act gay at the same time.

Thus conscience does make cowards of us all;

I didn't get the role in that play.

[TURNER removes the soft pack and replaces it in the paper bag.]

7. Sink or Swim

[Object: Floaties.]

[TURNER spends each paragraph break blowing up a child's inflatable swimming device.]

It's probably an understatement to say that I feel out of place from time to time, but I never saw it coming that I would feel so out of place in the queer community.

As an adult, I was raised by lesbians, you know, on organic lentils and feminist thought, and most days now people look at me and see a gay man if they're looking.

Coming out as transgender in the community that invented coming out, I've met with more resistance than I ever imagined possible.

Seriously—straight people seem to have very little problem with me. Yes, it was straight people who rallied hard to keep me female—I was just so pretty, you know—but now that I'm a guy, well, that makes sense. Now.

Gay people rallied for me to have the right to choose who I want to be, they've been doing it for all of us long before I was born. But now...if I'm not gay or lesbian, I find I have no brother's keeper. Even though, as a straight but transgender man, I'll always be pretty queer to the people who would pass laws excluding me, or to those who would, I don't know, murder me.

[Holding tight to the floatie, TURNER falls into the mattress like it's a pool.]

You just can't go throwing a queer kid into the straight end of the swimming pool like that! I want my queers! I want the people who held me up, who gave me the breath to speak my truth. These waters of being a straight guy—whether you're new to them or not—they're harder to navigate than you think.

[At the end of the last story, TURNER signals for the tissu to fall in from the audience. A voice message sounds while TURNER takes off his clothes, and then binds his chest with an ACE bandage and puts on boxers.]

[V.O.:]

Monday September 26th at 2:28pm:
Hey Scott—Listen, good news is that I've talked with the doc, and we're ready to write you a script. So I need to hear from you when you get a chance. I'll give you more info when we talk. Anyway, I look forward to speaking with you, and I hope that you feel some relief after this message.

ACT II

This is the part of the show where the middle should go. And I have to say, I really hate being in the middle. And I'm a Libra, so that's actually really difficult for me.

Back when I was in the middle, the psychiatrist I had to see so I could get testosterone told me he thought I might be bi–polar. Of course I could see that as possible, given the high swings of every caffeinated day, and the daily tragedies of humanity you get on the evening news; not to mention that we are constantly negotiating all of our pasts and every possible future. Who doesn't feel a little...out of sorts from time to time?

I think he was just calling me crazy because he didn't understand what I was going through. Maybe he did, but it seemed worrisome. He thought the middle might be safer. Swinging is dangerous; going all the way to one side is too much. More stability in the middle.

[TURNER climbs on the tissu. He ties it into a knot and begins to swing, small swings at first, building and building until he almost–dangerously swings from audience to audience at each edge of the ¾ thrust. Visually, two streams of text are projected over TURNER, one falling down, the other rising slowly; question after question after question from the time when he was In The Middle. As they pour down over him, he sings his own rendition of Leonard Cohen's "Bird on a Wire".]

[Falling down:]

What if this isn't what I want?
What if this isn't what I need?
What if my family disowns me?
How will I ever get another date?
What if testosterone kills me?
What if I don't like my body after surgery?
What if nobody will love me anymore?
Am I the weirdest person in the world?
What if I won't love myself?

Am I crazy to think this could be normal?
What if I get cancer and die?
What if they botch a surgery?
What if I come through, and want to go back?
What if I die?
What if I die?
What if I die?
What will I find?
Where will I find myself
if I don't know myself anymore?
What if I die?
When will I know what I want?
When will I know who I am?
When?
When will I know?

[Rising slowly:]

The truth about this whole gender thing
is that it's the thread of my entire life.
Few people get so lucky as to know
what they want
and have the resources to achieve it,
frightening though it may be.
Denial is a lie living ignored
and commitment to the truth,
some truth, a good truth
makes a good life. So I've been told.
So I want to believe.
What's the worst that could happen?
What cannot be undone?
And this path,
even if I double back
or return to the beginning,
it's a path of experience,
it winds and hopefully is long.
There is nothing wrong
with chasing after your life.

[Still swinging, stopped singing.]

I saw the psychiatrist picking up pie for
Thanksgiving a year after I started testosterone,
eleven months after I stopped seeing him. He said,
"You look well," and I said,

"Yeah, it's good from where I'm standing."

[TURNER comes down off the tissu. He puts on a suit that is at least 5 sizes too big for him while a voicemail plays:]

[V.O.:]

Okay, I'm outta the shower. Here's the question: Um, do boobs—girl boobs—produce hormones? Female hormones? Cuz, I asked Kate, and she's totally stumped by this, too. Um, I am breaking out like insanity on my jawline where most boys I know who start T get a lot of acne. I never, ever have ever broken out like this. It looks like, honestly it looks like I just started testosterone. So, anyway, I can't say that I've had a masque on before, at any rate it was a little traumatic, and then it got all over my phone when I was talking to you, and then I was afraid that you would go tell everybody, or put it on the Internet or something...

[At the end of of the voicemail, the image of the decoder ring is projected, indicating that it's time for more stories.]

STORY SECTION II

1. Have Many Happy Returns of the Day

[Object: Three birthday cards from 2003, 2004, and 2005.]

[All Action. TURNER reads 3 birthday cards sent to him by his mother and step–father.]

1) Daughter: I've seen so many different sides of you and loved every one of them...
But there's something very special about seeing who you are today—the wonderful woman I knew you'd be all along. Happy Birthday. Happy Birthday, Katie! Love, Mom and Chris.

2) To my son <and my little girl, Kt> who sometimes makes me nervous...

But always makes me proud. Happy Birthday.
We love you, Kt, and will be thinking of you in
Laramie on the Twelfth. When we see you next here,
we'll celebrate your birthday properly. Love, always,
Mom and Chris.

3) [Featuring the back of a naked child wearing just a
cowboy hat.]

Happy birthday to a son who's outgrown doing cute
things like this...You HAVE outgrown this, haven't
you, Son?
TURNER—this is the perfect card for you! Hope you
have a lovely birthday! It must be, your mother's
been laughing at it for a week! Happy Birthday. Lots
of love, Mom and Chris.

2. Listen to Your Heart

[Object: Pink Spalding ball.]

[TURNER bounces the ball rhythmically while he roams
the stage, walking the same flow that blood takes
through the heart.]

Some nights my heart beats so hard it keeps me
awake. This is not romantic. It's not metaphorical.
Something about the masculinization of my heart
with the introduction of testosterone; achieving my
earliest heart's desire in becoming a man makes me
more likely to die of heart disease, a heart attack.
Like my heart hasn't been attacking me since I
remember being aware.

Sometimes I think I must be disordered to take this
on, take this in, to stay awake at night listening to
my heart pounding, telling me I'm living. Living as a
man.

My heart is a man telling me I'm living my dream by
keeping me awake with his knocking in the night.

[TURNER bounces the ball twice more, then lets it
bounce away.]

3. Tie a Tie

[Object: A tie.]

[All action. TURNER ties a tie as fast as he can while audience hums the theme to *Jeopardy!*]

4. Change Your Name

[Object: Name change papers.]

On January Fourth, 2005, I stood before a judge and changed my name legally. Myself and five women from the tri–county area each enjoyed this simple but powerful legal transformation on this particular Thursday, extracting ourselves out from under the thumb of The Man, name first. The Man in my case being The Intransigent Social System Which Conflates Sex with Gender and Will Not Let Me Be Who I Am; The Man in the case of each of these women, their Ex–Husbands. Differentiate as you will.

Now, I am judged and found unworthy of manhood in the checkout line, I don't need to formalize the process. But it had to be done: Try as I might, I could not take the femininity out of my given name, "Katie." Just to make things interesting, I decided to do it in Texas.

Yes. Texas.

We assembled, my five lady friends and I, before the judge. Emotional exchanges about alimony and paternity had been echoing off the hallowed walls of justice for a good half hour, and continued, whispered over shoulder pads and the backs of chairs, in between decrees. My hands poured sweat as I sat in my dress slacks and tie. For all I knew, they might think I was one of them, a minion of The Man.

"Katie Lauren Kilborn," the judge calls. I rise, and make my way to the stand. As he watches me approach, he laughs, "You need a name change, donchya, Son."

"Yes, Sir. It might be a little more complicated than that, though."

"Well, let's see it." He treats me differently than the women who have come before. I know this undeserved kinship will soon shatter with his stare. I present the judge with two different orders.

[TURNER retrieves the orders from the audience.]

The first is one to change both name and gender designation; the second, just in case, was a simple name change. The judge takes a good long look at the first order, then eyes me, then glances back at the paper. Then, back to me. Then, back to the paper. "Unusual case. I don't think I've ever actually seen this before."

He's the kind of man you'd expect a judge to be. I mean, *of course*, he's white and male, but he's also silver-haired and broad-shouldered. Perhaps he was once athletic, though he seems too tall for a football player, too thick for baseball. I imagine him playing basketball for Baylor.

He picks up one of the law references on his desk and thumbs through.

"To be honest with you, I don't even know where I might find a precedent. Nope. It's not under gender. Darn it."

The court has fallen silent. I feel ten eyes, magnified with the fury of women scorned, sizing me up from behind, ten ears pricked up in interest.

The judge looks me over, but not in the way most people do when they consider what it means to have a transgender person standing in front of them. I don't feel his eyes on my chest or my crotch; he frames my shoulders, looks into my face and eyes. I hope my tie is straight: Suddenly the appearance of the knot is all that stands between me and that M on my driver's license. If only I had gone for the Windsor Knot instead of the Four in Hand!

"I just don't think I have the authority to do this kind of thing," he tells me. "I can't decree that somebody can be something...else. If I did, you'd have people changing their identities all the time..." He looks at me, it seems, for help.

I reply that I know a few people who have done it... That it seems a change in gender designation is, in fact, up to the judge's discretion. That he could even write, "Petitioner may not marry a person of the female sex" before he signed it, just to be covered in a sticky gay marriage situation. My judge frowns. "I want you to know that I know this isn't just some decision you made lightly. I know that you have to...undergo...many things to do this, and I don't have any problem with that. In fact, if I knew that there was some case law somewhere, I'd do it. I really would. But as it stands now, I just don't believe I can."

I tell him I understand, and say I'll find out for him, that I'll be back.

"Well, do you want to change your name? I can do that for you, at least." It feels almost like I'm a neighbor to whom he, upon finding a would–be borrowed lawnmower out of gas, offers at least a weed–whacker with which to attempt the job. From behind I hear a divorcée whisper, "I think I just saw this on Oprah!"

He swears me in, "So help me God." It goes on record in the State of Texas that I am changing my name as part of my gender transition and that each of those names reflects my family history. When I say the words "sex change" into the record, my judge blinks reflexively.

Finally, he adjudicates, orders, and decrees me Scott Turner Schofield, and as I exit past the five silent women he calls out, "Good luck, Son."

5. Get a Little Tiffany

[Prop: Cufflinks.]

When I graduated from college, a lesbian couple who are friends of my mom took me out to dinner. Halfway through I left the table, and when I came back, a Tiffany's bag stood all bright turquoise and expensive in front of my plate.

Oh, *shit*. I'd just come out as trans, and I thought they knew, but here I stood confronted with probably the latest Bean or Heart or whatever necklace bauble says, "I'm Privileged" (not that I keep track of status symbols). I gritted my teeth into my best girl smile over the preemptive guilt of knowing there was no way in hell this expensive gift would ever see the light of day, and I opened the box:

To find a pair of cufflinks, my initials engraved, and a card that read:

Because Every Woman Deserves a Little Tiffany in His Life.

6. Find Your Karaoke Anthem

[Prop: Microphone.]

You gotta find your karoake anthem, right? Please enjoy this musical selection while imagining that you are all straight people, that my voice has just broken and that we are in a bar in Cedar Rapids, Iowa.

[The karaoke version of Dusty Springfield's "Son of a Preacher Man" begins to play. The words that scroll on the sheet read differently:]

My mother tells me that
starting at age two,
she would dress me in dresses
and I would kick and fuss.

I can only see this
preverbal complaint
as my spirit
desiring expression.

Forget science or social construction
a screaming two–year–old
doesn't genetically hate dresses
or see them as symbols
of the patriarchy.

I feel my spirit stronger in sex.
Nothing about my glittery
rubber dildo
says biology.
It's not a prosthetic
nor does it,
by itself,
make me feel
like a "real man."

It's in the sex,
the fucking
inside all of that desire and pressure.
I can feel every inch,
and this sensation pleasures us both.
She says she feels me cum,
a hot blast inside of her
as I arch and moan
in my orgasm.

I've made her late for her period!

But there's nothing fluid
or immaculate
about it.

Only spirit,
expressing desire.

7. Break Hearts

[Prop: Receipt.]

I found this receipt with the name of a woman I once loved typed on it.

It wasn't anything cosmic. We had used her Safeway card to buy ingredients for a pie. Still, it was shocking to see her name coming out of my pocket in the laundromat down the street months after we had stopped seeing one another.

I wasn't telling the truth, the whole truth, nothing but the truth when I was with her. I thought my love for her was all the truth I needed; what did it matter that I loved another woman too, was loving her concurrently even as we made pie in this woman's kitchen?

My greatest fear is of becoming my father, my father the philanderer who had married seven times the last I counted and always has a girlfriend. Or even my grandfather who for over twenty years loved the woman next door better than his own wife. Do cheating hearts get passed down genetically, or is betrayal a language you learn from the silences in your home?

[Tearing the receipt into smaller and smaller squares.]

On the calendar you could call it the last thing I did as a woman, or the first thing I did as a man, but either way I was a sucky human being. I had an affair. I lied, and I broke two hearts. It fits, then, that mine should have been broken twice. First by one, then by the other. They said, "Here's your fucking love you cheap bastard, trying to get two for one. No refunds, no returns."

8. Live. Change.

[Object: Egg timer.]

[TURNER sets the egg timer, then creates a couch out of the cushions on the bed.]

People tell me I make this whole transition thing seem so easy, like a round of jokes I play on the world or take in with a sense of humor when the joke's on me. I haven't told you everything at all. I haven't told you about how I became deeply depressed at age eleven because I stopped being able to express myself as the boy I knew I was; how that silence grew and grew so I couldn't say anything at all; and I felt like I was choking so I tried to kill myself twice in high school and once since then, so I'd at least be dead and not just slowly dying. Of course it isn't easy. Sometimes I don't leave the house for days because I don't want any more absurd gender stories to happen to me. Some days I'm glad I can pass unnoticed as a man, and I just wish I didn't know the difference.

But knowing that my life is all just things that happen—stories that happen and end—made me know that I don't want to die, not really ever and especially not anytime soon. It's not death I want. It's change.

[The egg timer ticks loudly for what feels like too long.]

It's uncomfortable, huh? Waiting for change.

[When the egg timer rings, a voice message sounds while TURNER peels off the large suit, revealing the sharp blue suit underneath:]

[V.O.:]

Hey BooBoo, it's Bear. I've just spent the week in Jamestown, New York, the birthplace of Lucille Ball, and she's everywhere. Anyway, it's made me think a lot about gender and I've decided that a person is either a Lucy or a Ricky. You, my friend, are most certainly a Lucy. Give me a call and I'll tell you all about it.

ACT III

[TURNER takes the tissu and begins building a new fort, just for himself, center stage.]

When I was a kid and I built forts with other girls, we'd tell our parents we were just going to tell stories there. I never told any stories! My childhood forts were bachelor pads of discovery.

I made my first fort for Jennifer. She was 8, and I was 5, but mature, and she had hit puberty way early. She had the body of a woman, and boy, did she love me. She called me her best boy, and I would build a fort, and she would take my hand and lead me in and kiss me for hours of heat, friction, new exciting body parts and bliss.

I don't know if Jennifer thought I was a boy or just liked the kind of boy I was.

[TURNER enters the fort, lighting it from within with a flashlight. The fabric turns a sultry red.]

I brought a boy in here once. Me and this boy, we were best buds. We watched the movie *Alien* together. We were hot shit. I wanted to one–up him and trade knowledge and be schooled in the ways of boys. I invited him once into my fort and the first thing he says is, "You know you're a girl, right?" And I say, "No, I'm a boy, and what about my Darryl Strawberry card..." and he says, "Nuh–uh, I'm a boy, and you're a girl, and here's what that means."

Even after he showed me, I never thought I was a girl, I was just confused. Confused to know I had an inside.

[Abrupt light shift as TURNER appears out of the fort. He has no pants on, only child–size underoos.]

If you're wondering, and you might not be, but if you're wondering: I did not become a man because somebody made me feel bad for being a girl. Even within your own body, which is predetermined by genes and bones and parts, and then molded by people and what they do to you, you still happen any way you choose.

[Voice–over as TURNER disrobes completely again, then puts on some jeans, and sets to building a large and precarious fort out of the couch cushions. It will inevitably fall, over and over again, every time he tries.]

[V.O.:]

Hey Scott, it's Pat Graney, how you doin'? I just got your message about how you don't know how to be a man in 127 easy steps. Part of the process of making the piece is where you are now, and that will be great. You don't have to be wherever your ideal is of a man in order to write about it. That's the whole process that's so amazing. It's that you're going through what you're going through, and that needs to be part of your piece. And I think it's great. It's scary, it's like, "I don't know what I'm doing. I don't know how to be a man!" If you could save that message and listen to it again, it's like, "Of course not, because you're in the process of transition, and you always will be, it's not going to change. You're always going to be transitioning into something." So, I just want you to know that I just gave it some thought, and I just got out of therapy so I feel fairly well–balanced, and uh, that should be in your piece. How you freak out about it, how you think you have to be something, when there's nothing to be. Okay, bra? Cool. Call me later. Bye.

The last time I built my own fort, I was eleven years old. I tucked and rolled and strapped and folded, but found my body too big for a couch–cushion enclosure: Every move knocked or twisted something, and it all fell down. I cried in frustration. I cursed gravity! I was just too big anymore, and that's just how it goes. You get too big, and your world collapses around you, and you start again.

[TURNER pulls a black compression shirt from his jeans, pulls it on tight. His breasts flatten into pecs, his waist straightens into lines.]

My body tells my truth now, mostly, but the story is so big that sometimes I lie, just to keep the moment intact.

[A thin shaft of light shines in darkness. TURNER pulls down his jeans. In doing so, he finds a syringe in his pocket. He sits down so that the beam lights the injection site on his thigh. He holds the syringe in the light and injects himself as he speaks the following text:]

I was just shy of 25 when I stopped my own female process, stopping up the monthly flow of progesterone and estrogen with a syringe full of testosterone. Life in pain? Dream come true. Life in pain? Dream come true.

I penetrate myself every two weeks to change my insides, and my outsides, myself, and I will stick myself twice a month for the rest of my life, never knowing if I am giving myself life or bringing on a faster death. Life in pain? Dream come true?

[TURNER pulls up his jeans as slow-motion MRI footage is projected on the sheet. He begins to climb the tissu one final time, taking huge and sweeping steps up the fabric. As the voice-over ends, TURNER wraps into Angel Pose, the tissu holding him up and falling like long wings over his shoulders.]

[V.O.:]

When I die they'll take these organs from me and I hope they'll give them to somebody else. Except, I wonder if they segregate hearts, eyes, livers, and lungs by sex. And if they do, how will mine help the next body they're in?

There's this little pearl in your brain called the hypothalamus, it's just a few millimeters in size, and it controls the torrents of hormones that make you develop your vagina or your penis in utero, then your facial hair and your period during puberty. At least that's one story I heard. It's hard to believe because you can hardly see this little gland with your eye, and then I put barely a quarter teaspoon of a hormone into myself twice a month and my whole body—five feet ten, one hundred and fifty pounds, 206 bones, miles of intestine and skin—my whole body morphs so even my own mother barely recognizes it. The proportion of change feels impossible, mythic.

[The projection stops. A single beam lights TURNER high above the audience.]

[Spoken:]

In a hero myth, the hero ascends, becomes one with God or becomes godlike in knowledge and understanding. And then we have the Everyman story, where Everyman undergoes trials and learns something and becomes more of a man than ever. But I'm not going to imagine myself as either one of those men, because neither one would be quite right.

[TURNER falls, fast and acrobatic, like an accident which is, in truth, completely controlled. Then, grounded, he says:]

Me, Everyman?

One more story. My choice this time.

I'm the best babysitter ever because I'll tell just one more story, and I'll let you build forts in the living room. I'm sitting with my four–year–old friends Royce and Elsbeth, and Royce has known me since I was KT, the best girl babysitter ever. His parents have explained to him, "KT is a man now, and he wants you to call him TURNER. Do you have any questions?" Royce told them no, because he and I already have secret agent names, and it makes more sense that I've really been a boy all along. Kinda like in Scooby–Doo, when they pull off the mask.

But Elsbeth doesn't know about me. She's just here for dinner and a video. Just in the middle of making one last fort before dinner, Royce tells her, "Turner was a woman, but now he's a man. A MAAAAAAN!" Just like that. Then he looks up at me, and it occurs to him, "How did you do that?"

Elsbeth seems horrified. Forget about the gender confusion. I'm sure by this point she's been socialized not to ask prying questions, not to stare, not to point. Meanwhile, I am faced with the prospect of explaining transsexuality and gender identity to four–year–olds.

"Um, well, Royce, you see, you really...you really have to want it," I say, forgoing the anatomy book and flowchart route. This seems like a reasonable, clear response. You do have to really, really want it.
"I really, really want to be a woman," Royce tells us, completely unselfconscious and totally sure. "A WOOOOMAAAAN!!!" I tuck another corner of their couchback afghan and try to just let this moment happen, respect what the child says, believe, and affirm.

"What's a woman?" asks Elsbeth. My heart is pounding out of my chest, I can barely catch my breath, I just want to get inside the fort and tell a fucking ghost story that will scare them into next week so we can not be having this conversation! But they're both staring at me so damn intently. I say, "Um, well, ah, a woman is...a woman can be...anything, anybody can be a woman. So long as they're smart. And strong. Both you and Royce could be a woman because you are each both of those things. And you know, Elsbeth, I think lots of women would really like your shoes." (They're flip flops with a silk flower hot glued at the toe separator.) Elsbeth beams at the compliment.

"What about my shoes?" Royce cries. He's got these Velcro sneakers, the kind that light up at the back. "Oh I think a lot of women would really like those too. When I was a woman I would have worn those for sure. You see, women are all different, and you can choose who you want to be. You can be a woman or a man or something different, you can be anything you want, you could be...a..."

"Basketball player–crane operator!" they overlap.

I finish the fort. This should trump all talk of identity politics and feminist thought. They slide in. Then Elsbeth's muffled voice through the fabric:

"Come in here and tell us a stoooorreeeee. Tell us how you became a man!"

[TURNER breaks down the fort he has just constructed, and tells the audience:]

I wish I could tell you everything, but no matter how many stories I tell I can't figure out how to end this story that never really ends for me. All I know is what I've learned so far: Be a man about it. Look people in the eye, shake hands firmly, say thank you, and know when to leave.

[TURNER exits. Lights go down. He does not take a bow. When the audience leaves the theater, TURNER stands at the door and shakes their hands, one by one, and thanks them for listening.]

REALLY THIS TIME. THE END.

Turner presents with a diagnosis
Gender Identity Disorder (302.8
He meets all
criteria
this disorder
a str
not merely a

Are We There Yet?
Being and Becoming a
Transgender Performance Artist

An earlier version of this essay appeared in
Self–Organizing Men, edited by Jay Sennett, published by
Homofactus Press.

Peggy Shaw once turned to me in exasperation and said, "You really think there are answers, don't you?" I did. I do. And I am proved wrong over and over again.

I have named the curve of my waist, the one that stubbornly resists masculinity, my learning curve. You'll see it when I perform, before I take off my shirt to show you what's still there on my chest. My chest and my waist remind me—and tell you—that there are no truths when it comes to sex, gender, or sexuality: Only bodies, perception, and imagination.

I. Get Out the Map

I became a transgender performance artist because I am a gender–transgressive actor and writer who could not find work in mainstream theater. Rather than wait for the perfect role to come along, I began in 2000 to write a script for myself. As an actor, I wanted to know what it would be like to act a part I found meaningful. As an activist–minded artist, I wanted to tell a story I was not hearing about the transgender experience I found myself living. As a student of theater, I had been steeped in Shakespeare and Ibsen. Only after reading *O Solo Homo*, an anthology of queer solo performances, did I realize there was a whole iceberg of queer theater out there, while I stood on the mainstream theater boat, praying for a crash. Wild in the eyes and heart, I approached my queer literature professor, Julie Abraham, who had just seen me perform *As You Like It* in period dress. She suggested I show up at Pride in the dress that made me look like a geeky fag in drag as Queen Elizabeth I.

"This is the kind of theater I want to make!" I shouted.

Then I learned perhaps the most important lesson of my college career: There are only two degrees of separation in the queer community. If you don't know someone, someone you know knows someone who does. (Marginalization has its perks: This phenomenon is the reason you, Dear Reader, hold this book in your hands.) Dr. Abraham didn't even blink as she replied, "Oh, my best friend Esther Newton is Holly Hughes' partner, and she's working on a book. What are you doing this summer?"

During the summer of 2000, I landed a position as a research assistant to raucous lesbian performance artists Holly Hughes and Alina Troyano (a.k.a. Carmelita Tropicana), founding members of the WOW Café, a feminist (at the time, entirely lesbian and bisexual, but not, to my memory, trans) theater collective in New York City's East Village. They wanted to write a book to commemorate the 20th anniversary of the space. I was to serve as their on-the-scene reporter, questioning previous and current members about its history. The book never materialized, but my own aesthetic, and also my trans identity, took root during that summer.

In New York that year, I saw Sarah Jones' *Surface Transit* at P.S. 122— a brilliantly embodied solo performance on the complications of race and ethnicity—that impacted my thinking for what would become my first solo show, *Underground Transit*. I watched spoken word and drag king shows. I traveled to Rochester to watch *Menopausal Gentleman* and saw Peggy Shaw look as good in a suit as I could ever dream for myself. I spent my time at the WOW Café, where theater, for once, looked like my life. I also met the first person I ever knew to be a transman. I lived twelve blocks from Toys in Babeland. Holly Hughes and Carmelita Tropicana were my mentors. I rode the subway for days, seeing through culturally sheltered eyes an unknown world of class, race, and gender, all sweating upon one another during the evening rush hour. I was a dyke with a trannie–boy's life history, on my first summer away from home, just learning the difference between sex, sexuality, and gender identity. The drama wrote itself.

I returned home to Emory University in Atlanta to professors delighted by my new drive. The queer theorists I had read in Women's Studies told me that gender is a performance and that transpeople are transgressive actors on the stage of real life—could this be true? Could my story be told without using words like "ontology" and "performativity?" Could, say, my middle–American family understand that sex, gender, and sexuality are separate—that they are not fixed concepts? And would understanding this help them accept me? In *Gender Outlaw*, the perfect mix of gender theory and staged gender performance, Kate Bornstein wrote, "I look for theater that focuses on transformation, because I go along for the ride and am myself transformed." (162) I crossed the quad from Women's Dtudies to the theater building.

The same theater professors who could not find a role for me in seasons of traditional theater became important allies, reading drafts and giving notes at my rehearsals to help me create my best artistic work. Each of us was still learning how to define transgender identity. The lack of definition left me with only my own story to tell: The only appropriate mission after all. Onstage with just a backpack full of costumes, I began performing the ways in which a body can—and will—box itself and burst out of that box again and again. Judging by the audience response, those queer theorists were right: Gender is a performance. The magic of live theater made emotional sense out of intellectual theory.

I began touring before I graduated from college. A few students on Spring Break skipped a kegger to come see my show. They worked some student activity fee magic to bring me up to Bard College.

Students from other universities attended the show, and the ball kept rolling. In perfect grassroots organizing style, a solo performer living in the Deep South (not New York City) actually got a full-time gig performing feminist, activist theater around the country! What's that they say about life and art? I thought I had died and gone to a place where Jill Dolan is God, and the WOW Café is but the pearly gates to Heaven.

I performed *Underground Transit* for two years while I created my next show. In my life, I passed for a woman, and I passed for rich too, and these privileges brought me to not one, but three Debutante Balls. In *Debutante Balls*, the show, I tell the story of coming out at three Southern Galas, but never as a debutante. I was always the friend of the deb, the queer-looking one who obviously didn't come from money and once brought a black man as her escort. This peripheral perspective gave me all the room of a radical feminist queer nationalist peanut gallery from which to comment on the race, class, and gender issues inherent at those fancy parties—and to have some fun with it, too. The show was also an opportunity to make the South a living, modern, and complicated place in the audience's imagination—when since *Designing Women* went off the air has that happened?

In 2005, I gatecrashed the invitation-only National Performance Network Annual Meeting. Sometimes you gotta make your own access. The rebels at NPN were very welcoming. Sitting in the Queer Caucus gathering, the fabulous lesbian choreographer and world-famous prison arts pioneer Pat Graney said, "I think the most interesting queer work happening right now is being done by transgender artists. Scott, what do you know about this?" I was speechless in a good way: Somebody privileged trans art at a national meeting of arts presenters? What? Soon afterwards, Pat committed to a three year mentorship project, starting with a major commission for my next piece. How do you go from off-the-grid to funded and anticipated? In my experience, half-cocked.

I was ready to write a new show, but about what? I churned out 40 pages of pseudo–theoretical nonsense, less fun than my class lectures, but with nudity and better lighting. Kate Bornstein read it, called me, and simply said, "I hate it." Can you imagine? Just as I prepared to re–tie my server apron for good, she called back and said, "Just tell me a story."

I do so love our little chats.

My life was full of stories, many that didn't make it into my other shows, so many that I didn't know what to do with them all. But my metaphor well had run dry: How would I hang them all together?

"Okay," my partner–in–crime S. Bear Bergman sighed, as ze always does when calming me down on a late night, long distance phone call. "So you have about 127 stories to tell and an hour in which to make sex change EASY, step–by–step." I made notecards from memories, ruminated, and typed. Then I found one of my old *Choose Your Own Adventure* books from elementary school. Later, on tour in New York, T Cooper and Felicia Luna Lemus left Joe Meno's book *The Boy Detective Fails* by the couch they made up as a bed for me. There I found the decoder ring. With such random origins, how could I write any linear play? The elements of chance that structured my process had to be reflected in the product.

Okay, lest Oprah come knocking, I should tell you: The big lie in all of my truths is, I don't have 127 stories yet. While I intend *Becoming a Man...* to be my last solo show about my transgender identity, it will certainly be the Cher Farewell Tour of final performances. As I write this, I am 27–years–old, and as a man, I look about 20. I hope to live a long and happy life—if only to reverse the tragic dead tranny stereotype. I don't do anything anymore unless it will make a good story. So stay tuned.

II. All Signs Point To...?

Like most people, I struggle with labels. I feel I must describe, claim, and process all the social factors that make me who I am—proving that you can take the lesbian out of his body, but you can't take the lesbian out of the man. I tick off the list of Important Things I Learned in Women's Studies (race, sexuality, class, gender) to enact the message of my work: Come out as you are, whatever you are. Be specific, so that you see the many places where you connect to the bigger world around you. But for God's sake, have a sense of humor about it, so that you can live in that world.

But how do you market that? Since my transgender eureka moment back in 2000, I have struggled to identify myself not only to myself, but to paying audiences as well. I was born Katie Lauren Kilborn. I became—partly out of shorthand, but also because of some misguided idea it was gender neutral—Kt Kilborn. (I found everyone asking: "Kt? You mean like K–A–T–I–E?") How I became Scott Turner Schofield is detailed in *Becoming a Man in 127 EASY Steps*. For a while, I was a "lesbian skirting gender boundaries." Then I became a "Trannie boy–lesbian." Then a "dyke boy," and then, my favorite: A mix of carefully–timed she and he pronouns that tell my whole story.

"Consider your audience," my marketing mind coos. "Tell them what they want to hear." But my target audience is anyone with a gender and/or anyone who has ever felt different. That's everybody. But we live in a world where even my spellchecker still underlines the word transgender with wavy red lines. We do not possess language to integrate ourselves meaningfully either personally or in communities. How do you tell a coherent story with unfixed and problematic elements like sex, gender, and sexuality? How do you advertise that? How do you get a fratboy—who may or may not be queer or an ally, but who is negotiating gender, acceptance, and community (differently, but deeply) just like any transperson—to connect to a poster with the word "transgender" on it? Without that label, how do you bring in the queers and the allies? And since trans is not inherently queer anyway, and barely anybody goes to theater anymore, what difference does it make?

The only real answers I have have found are to make it extra credit for classes and "diversity credits" for the Greek system.

Also, make a big scene.

In May 2006, Central Piedmont Community College (CPCC) in Charlotte, North Carolina, canceled my performance of *Underground Transit*. This state funded institution gave me an ultimatum: End the show fully–clothed or take your transgender body and its performance to another venue. Their discomfort centered around whether taking my shirt off and showing my transgender chest, unmodified by surgery, but changed by hormones, constituted "obscene nudity."

A male actor playing Jesus in *Jesus Christ, Superstar* performed at CPCC in only a loincloth. But, as the CPCC venue manager said to the *Charlotte Observer*, "A man who has always been a man is different, I think. That's my own personal take on it."

I disrobe at the end of *Underground Transit* as a final act of vulnerability before my audience. The effect, I have been told, is one of recognizing a human body perpetually shrouded in sexualized mystery, with enough backstory to simply appreciate that body. It is not for shock value or titillation. This explanation, however, did not convince the higher–ups at CPCC.

In the end, I had to perform elsewhere in Charlotte. The media stink I created brought a huge and diverse audience to the show to form their own opinions. CPCC's venue manager even sat in the front row.

III. We're on the Road to Nowhere

I began injecting testosterone in October 2005. The documentary *TransGeneration* and the movie *TransAmerica* simmered mainstream interest in transgender issues already heated by the antics of Rikki Wilchins, et al., and Hilary Swank's Oscar nod for *Boys Don't Cry*. My booking line started ringing more often. My voice dropped about an octave in six weeks.

In late November, I performed at a state college in the Northeast. The show was packed. From the floor to standing, the room filled with the "perfect audience" I always seek: Visible queers alongside sorority girls, jocks, worried administrators, and eager professors. For the first time since my voice dropped, I asked the crowd, "Would you believe I was almost Homecoming Queen in high school?" A loud guffaw shot out from a man in the third row, which he attempted to cover with a cough. Titters arose from the rest. Eyes squinted. My audience checked me out from ass to chest to throat to crotch as I told them the story.

About two–thirds through, as I undress to reveal my bound breasts, a huge jock stalked across the performance space to the exit. He called me a faggot as he left. I happened to be singing "Boys Don't Cry" at that moment. I could not write these moments. I have since considered planting someone to reenact that unplanned moment at every show (can you imagine how many allies were born in that moment?), except my writer brain says it's too unbelievable, too mired in stereotype to actually sound true.

During the post–show Q&A, someone finally asked the lingering question I could feel, but couldn't find. "So, you were born...what? A boy or a girl? I can't tell." I realized suddenly that for some in this audience, I had skipped woman entirely. Even though I performed the piece with exactly the same words and costumes as I did before undergoing medical transition, they heard transgender, saw a body that looked and sounded like a man's, and through the same story I'd been telling for five years, I passed into transwoman—MTF, not FTM. I never realized that my personal gender journey would leave me unable to tell my own transgender story.

Did I genderfuck myself out of my own fucking gender?

At the time of this printing, the first line of my bio describes me as "a man who was a woman, a lesbian turned straight guy (who is mostly perceived as a gay boy)." Is it possible to just be trans in the moment, without explanation? Or is storytelling, to myself and others, the condition of being—and staying—transgender?

To some transpeople I know, revealing my truths through story makes me less of a "real man." To others (gay, lesbian, bi, queer, as well as straight), I will never be a "real man" no matter how convincing my story nor how skilled my portrayal. That opinion makes me forever just an actor in my own life.

Sometimes I fantasize about leaving this career, assuming another new name, and living my straight guy identity in Hollywood. I could become the next [fill-in-the-blank with your favorite male movie star. Who I am to dictate your desire?]!

In my fantasy, the night before I was to be featured as *People Magazine's* Sexiest Man Alive, I would come out. I would probably never work again—they're big on believability in Hollywood—but wouldn't it make a great story? You'd come out to see that solo theater show, wouldn't you?

Acknowledgements

For deep and numerous reasons, I thank:

Mom and Chris, and Carey Martin.

My trans artist family: Ryka Aoki, S. Bear Bergman, Kate Bornstein, T Cooper, Sean Dorsey, Imani Henry, Katz/Athens Boys Choir, Angela Motter, and the Tranny Roadshow.

Vincent Murphy and Alice Benston.

Steve Bailey.

Other artists of profound influence: Loren Cameron, DAH Teatar, Melissa Foulger, Pat Graney, Sarah Jones, Felicia Luna Lemus, Tony Kushner, Katharine (McElroy) Manasco, GiGi Monroe, the Neo-Futurists, Topher Payne, Amy Ray, Peggy Shaw, Alina Troyano, Lois Weaver, and Amy Wheeler.

Every technician who has ever loaned their magic to my stage.

The following theaters, individuals, and organizations that have been instrumental in the development of my work: John D. Leistler; Theater Emory, every single person at Theater Studies at Emory University from 1998–2002; Angelika Bammer; Ha Jin, Joseph Skibell, Jim Grimsley, and Natasha Trethewey; Jody Usher; Linda Bryant and the amazing feminists at Charis Books & More; Anna Millman; Cliterati; Estrofest Productions; Alternate ROOTS; Weir Harmon and Actor's Express; Sheri Mann Stewart and Barry Stewart Mann; the Playwriting Center at Emory; the Tanne Foundation; Cia Ricco at Rancho la Vida del Corazòn; Jump-Start Performance Company; The Pat Graney Company; Sixto Wogan at DiverseWorks; Alison Hastings and

Roy Peter Clark; Kate Warner; Polly Carl and The Playwrights' Center in Minneapolis; Toby Boshak, Ted Rawlins, and the Princess Grace Foundation-USA; and Del Hamilton and the 7 Stages family.

Jack Halberstam. Thank you especially for lending your commitment and hard work to my words here.

My private donors.

My brilliant volunteer book designer and friend, Charlie Burnett at www.madrabbitgraphics.com.

My fastidious proofreader and friend, Anne Lynch.

The valiant volunteer staff of Homofactus Press for your enthusiasm, your vision, and for making me a part of your important history.

Bibliography and Photo Credits

"Trouble Yum" performed by Three Finger Cowboy, written by Katharine McElroy. *Hooray for Love.* Daemon Records. 1999. Used by permission.

"Baby I'm a Star" performed by Three Finger Cowboy, written by Katharine McElroy. *Hooray for Love.* Daemon Records. 1999. Used by permission.

"Cradle and All" written and performed by Ani DiFranco. *Not a Pretty Girl.* Righteous Babe Records, 1995.

"Mtns of Glory" written and performed by Amy Ray. *Stag.* Daemon Records. 2001. Used by permission.

Marling, Karal Ann. *Debutante: Rites and Regalia of American Debdom.* Lawrence: University Press of Kansas, 2004.

Shakespeare, William. "Hamlet." *Shakespeare: The Complete Dramatic and Poetic Works of William Shakespeare Red Letter Edition.* Intr. Frederick D. Losey. Philadelphia: John C. Winston Company, 1952. 1000–1040.

Bornstein, Kate. *Gender Outlaw: On Men, Women, and the Rest of Us.* New York: 1st Vintage Books ed. 1995.

Photo Credits are, in order:

Judith Halberstam photo by Asaf Evron.

All candid and personal photos used by permission of the subjects.

Production photo from Underground Transit by Alex White. Taken at the PushPush Theater, Atlanta. Estrofest Productions, 2002.

Production photo from Debutante Balls by Ann Borden. Taken at Emory University.

Production photo from Becoming a Man in 127 EASY Steps by Elliat Graney-Sauke. Taken at the Capitol Hill Arts Center, Seattle. The Pat Graney Company, 2007.

Back cover photo by Maximillian Corwell, 2007.

About Scott Turner Schofield

Scott Turner Schofield is a man who was a woman, a lesbian turned straight guy (who is mostly read as a gay teenager), creating theater about gender and sexuality from within the Deep South. Schofield began his performance art career working as a research assistant to Holly Hughes and Carmelita Tropicana at the WOW Café in 2000. Now a full-time performance artist, educator, and producer, he tours his acclaimed one-trannie shows to colleges, theaters and festivals nationwide.

His solo work has been selected for programming at such venues as HERE Arts Center, the Philadelphia Fringe Festival, New York City's Fresh Fruit Festival at the Cherry Lane Theater, the Chicago Single File Festival, 7 Stages in Atlanta, Seattle's Pat Graney Company, San Antonio's Jump-Start Performance Company, FRESH MEAT in San Francisco, Yale Cabaret, as well as at scores of colleges and universities.

Schofield is the youngest recipient ever of a Tanne Foundation Award for Outstanding Achievement and Commitment to Art. In 2007, he became the first openly transgender artist to be commissioned by the National Performance Network for "Becoming a Man in 127 EASY Steps." He is an Artistic Associate at 7 Stages in Atlanta, thanks to a 2007 Princess Grace Foundation Fellowship in Acting.

He is truly grateful that you read this far and wishes you the inspiration necessary to transition as much and as often as you like, and the guts to be nice to yourself and others while you do.

About Homofactus Press

Homofactus Press, LLC began as a concept of Jay Sennett, noted filmmaker, writer, speaker, and blogger and has emerged as a small, digital publishing company. Homofactus Press primarily publishes books directed at female-to-male transsexuals / transmen / transgenders (FtMs) throughout the United States, Canada, Great Britain and Australia.

The mission of Homofactus Press is to publish the highest quality of books that discuss meaningful experiences by, for, and about FtMs, with particular emphasis towards communities of color and communities with disabilities.

To learn more about us, please visit http://www.homofactuspress.com

Printed in the United States
154217LV00009B/79/P